P · O · C · K · E · T · S

CARS

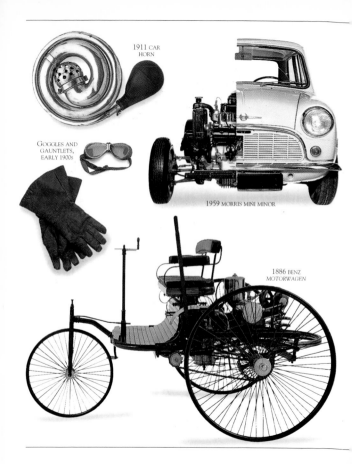

1911 CAR HORN

GOGGLES AND GAUNTLETS, EARLY 1900s

1959 MORRIS MINI MINOR

1886 BENZ MOTORWAGEN

P · O · C · K · E · T · S

CARS

Written by
GORDON CRUICKSHANK

ROLLS-ROYCE
"FLYING
LADY", U.K.

FIAT BADGE, ITALY

CASE BADGE, U.S.A.

1934 FORD SEDAN

DORLING KINDERSLEY
London • New York • Stuttgart

A DORLING KINDERSLEY BOOK

Project editors	Steve Setford
	Miranda Smith
Art editor	Sarah Crouch
Designer	Sarah Cowley
Senior editor	Hazel Egerton
Senior art editor	Jacquie Gulliver
Picture research	Fiona Watson
Production	Ruth Cobb
Additional text	John Farndon

First published in Great Britain in 1995
by Dorling Kindersley Limited
9 Henrietta Street, Covent Garden, London WC2E 8PS

Copyright © 1995 Dorling Kindersley Ltd., London

A CIP catalogue record for this book is available from
the British Library

ISBN 0 7513 5323 X

Colour reproduction by Colourscan, Singapore
Printed and bound in Italy by L.E.G.O.

CONTENTS

HOW TO USE THIS BOOK

These pages show you how to use *Pockets: Cars*. The book is divided into several parts. The main section gives detailed information about hundreds of cars. There is also an introductory section at the front, and a reference section at the back.

ALL ABOUT THE CARS
The cars in the book have been grouped into eight sections. An introductory page at the beginning of each section gives an overview of the pages that follow. Turn to the contents or index pages for more information.

CORNER CODING
Corners of the main section pages are colour coded to remind you which section you are in.

- INSIDE THE CAR
- LUXURY CARS
- EVERYDAY CARS
- SPORTS CARS
- SPECIALIST CARS
- RACING CARS
- CLASSIC CARS
- INTO THE FUTURE

Heading

Corner coding

Introduction

Caption

SPORTS CARS

ROAD RACERS

WHAT MAKES a sports car? The earliest "sport were ordinary cars stripped down to the basic maximum speed. Later, were sleek tourers in by such racing techn the supercharger. Tot sports car can be a 3. (200 mph) monster stylish 660cc "runab

ROAD RACER
Mercedes used a strong, light frame in the 300SL, making it ideal for racing. It won at Le Mans in 1952.

1957 MERCEDES-BENZ 300SL
The futuristic "Gullwing" could do 212 km/h (144 mph), but had little luggage space.

Engine fitted in streamlined low bonnet

All-independent suspension

Annotation

HEADING
This describes the subject of the page. This page is introducing sports cars. If a subject continues over several pages, the same heading applies.

INTRODUCTION
This provides a clear, general overview of the subject. After reading the introduction, you should have an idea of what the pages are about.

LABELS
For extra clarity, some pictures have labels. These give extra information, or identify a picture when it is not obvious from the text what it is.

RUNNING HEADS

These remind you which section you are in. The top of the left-hand page gives the section name. The top of the right-hand page gives the subject. The page called "Road racers" is in the Sports Cars section.

FACT BOXES

Many pages in the introductory and main sections have fact boxes. These contain at-a-glance information and provide extra facts about the subject. The fact box on "Road racers" gives interesting details about sports cars.

Running head

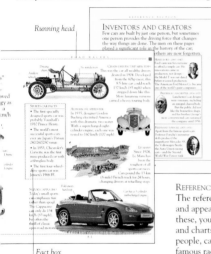

Fact box

REFERENCE SECTION

The reference section pages are yellow and appear at the back of the book. On these, you will find useful facts, figures, and charts, including a timeline of people, cars, and events, and details of famous races and amazing car records.

CAPTIONS AND ANNOTATIONS

Each illustration has a caption, and many have annotations. The annotations, in *italics*, point out features of an illustration and they are usually connected to a particular part of the illustration by a leader line.

INDEX

The index at the back of the book lists subjects alphabetically. There is also an alphabetical glossary that explains the meanings of the technical terms used in the book.

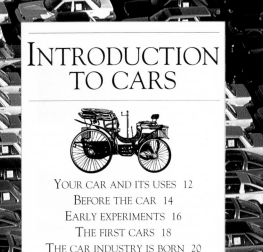

INTRODUCTION
TO CARS

YOUR CAR AND ITS USES

YOUR CAR IS AN everyday marvel. Instead of queuing in the rain for buses, you can drive door-to-door and stay warm and dry. It costs no more to move five people than one, and the car offers freedom for the disabled and security for the vulnerable. But there is an environmental price for luxury.

SUNDAY RITUAL
In the 1930s, merely owning a vehicle gave status, and much love was lavished on the family car.

ALL ABOARD
We do not think twice about loading our cars with equipment for an outdoor adventure holiday. But imagine trying to manage this by public transport!

TARMAC DESERT
City parking is getting very difficult, so new shops and cinemas are often located outside the built-up areas, where huge car-parks can be laid out. This uses up ever more countryside, and has, in fact, changed the suburban landscape.

AUTO-MOBILITY
A car can offer much-needed independence to someone who has difficulty getting about. This lady's wheelchair swings up into the car without her getting out of it.

Owner servicing her own car

Range of tools for hire

DO-IT-YOURSELF
Once, you had to be able to fix your car whenever and wherever it broke down. Now, most cars are extremely reliable, and breakdown services can usually sort out most problems quickly. However, as servicing costs rise, there is also the option of DIY workshops, where you can hire tools and hoists, and get expert advice.

BEFORE THE CAR

UNTIL THE INVENTION of the wheel more than 5,000 years ago, people made journeys on foot or on animals such as horses or donkeys. New forms of transport emerged as many countries became industrialized in the 18th and 19th centuries. In the 1820s, the birth of the railways brought cheap travel to the public.

PEDAL POWER
Cycling became a popular leisure activity in the late 19th century.

TRANSPORT BY CANAL
Canals have existed for thousands of years. Horse-drawn barges were an efficient, if slow, way to move goods, because a horse can pull far more through water than it can carry or pull on land.

EARLY TRAINS
Steam trains were faster than travel on horseback, but the open wagons made the journey uncomfortable and dirty. By the 1850s, passengers could travel in comfort at speeds of up to 95 km/h (60 mph).

Carriage carried on wagon

Double-decker passenger carriage

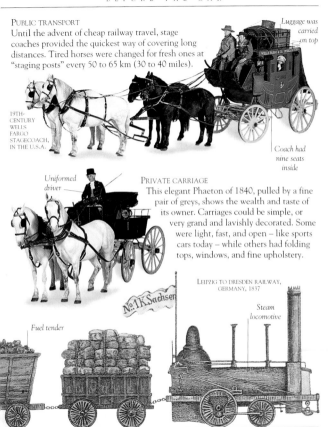

PUBLIC TRANSPORT

Until the advent of cheap railway travel, stage coaches provided the quickest way of covering long distances. Tired horses were changed for fresh ones at "staging posts" every 50 to 65 km (30 to 40 miles).

Luggage was carried on top

19TH-CENTURY WELLS FARGO STAGECOACH, IN THE U.S.A.

Coach had nine seats inside

Uniformed driver

PRIVATE CARRIAGE

This elegant Phaeton of 1840, pulled by a fine pair of greys, shows the wealth and taste of its owner. Carriages could be simple, or very grand and lavishly decorated. Some were light, fast, and open – like sports cars today – while others had folding tops, windows, and fine upholstery.

LEIPZIG TO DRESDEN RAILWAY, GERMANY, 1837

Steam locomotive

No. 1 K.Sachsen

Fuel tender

EARLY EXPERIMENTS

PEOPLE DREAMED of self-propelled machines for years before they were invented. In the 1800s, steam quickly proved the most successful system, but was better suited to public transport. Several crucial inventions had to come together before a car reached the road – the four-stroke engine, liquid fuel, and electric ignition.

BATTERY-DRIVEN
The early attempts at making machines move included this tricycle.

FIRST CAR FACTS

• Richard Trevithick built a steam carriage in Cornwall in 1801.
• Belgian Etienne Lenoir perfected an internal combustion engine that burned coal-gas in 1860.

CUGNOT
The first self-propelled vehicle that actually worked was Nicholas Cugnot's steam *Fardier*, built in 1769 to tow French army guns. Slow and unwieldy, it remained an experiment.

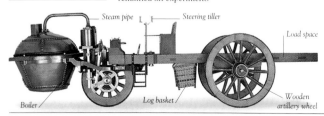

Steam pipe — Steering tiller

Load space

Boiler

Log basket

Wooden artillery wheel

CHAOS

In the first half of the 18th century, steam transport was unpopular because of its noise and smoke. Cartoonist Alken foresaw pollution and accidents when, in 1830, he imagined London's roads crowded with new-fangled machines.

Sprung coach body above cylinders

Stoker sits behind boiler

BORDINO STEAM CARRIAGE

This elaborate steam coach, built in 1852 in Italy by Virginio Bordino, survives today in the Biscaretti Musuem in Turin. It ran quite successfully, but at that time, steam was simply too clumsy and dangerous for use on the public roads.

Coal-gas engine under seat

Iron-shod wooden wheels

PIONEER MOTORIST

This car built by Austrian inventor Siegfried Marcus is thought to date from 1885. The first car reported to have been powered by an internal-combustion engine is on display at the Vienna Technical Museum.

THE FIRST CARS

THE FIRST PROPER motor-cars were invented by two Germans. Gottlieb Daimler devised a petrol motor which he fitted to a crude wooden cycle in 1885. Nearby, at almost the same time, Karl Benz built a complete car, and began selling new models two years later.

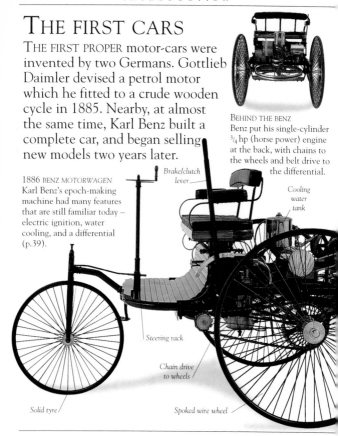

BEHIND THE BENZ
Benz put his single-cylinder ³/₄ hp (horse power) engine at the back, with chains to the wheels and belt drive to the differential.

1886 BENZ MOTORWAGEN
Karl Benz's epoch-making machine had many features that are still familiar today – electric ignition, water cooling, and a differential (p.39).

Brake/clutch lever

Cooling water tank

Steering rack

Chain drive to wheels

Solid tyre

Spoked wire wheel

THE SYSTÈME PANHARD

WORKING TOGETHER
René Panhard and Emile Levassor's influential partnership changed the look of the motor-car. Their *Système Panhard* (front engine, central gearbox, and rear-wheel drive) was adopted by most manufacturers from the 1890s onwards.

EARLY WARNING
Noisy, smelly automobiles were disliked by riders and carters, as horses often bolted. For a few years, in Britain, the law required a man with a red flag to precede any powered vehicle, and imposed a 6 km/h (4 mph) speed limit.

Face-to-face seating

PEUGEOT'S TWIN-CYLINDER
Peugeot's first cars used Daimler's engines, but in 1896 Peugeot developed its own twin-cylinder. It powered advanced four-seaters with sparkless ignition. The face-to-face seating and underfloor engine soon disappeared.

BURST OF STEAM
Petrol had its rivals, too. New technology brought efficient steam cars like this 1903 White. These cars burned kerosene, and needed no gear-changes – a big advantage over their petrol rivals.

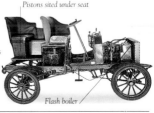

Pistons sited under seat

Flash boiler

THE CAR INDUSTRY IS BORN

IN THE EARLY 1900s, demand for cars rose rapidly. Most
were expensively hand-built, but some manufacturers
realized that the more they could build, the more they
could sell. Also, with
mass production and
assembly-line factories,
the price of cars
decreased and
more people
could afford
to buy them.

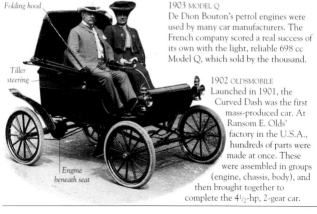

Wheel steering

Engine at front of car

Wooden spokes

Folding hood

Tiller steering

Engine beneath seat

1903 MODEL Q
De Dion Bouton's petrol engines were
used by many car manufacturers. The
French company scored a real success of
its own with the light, reliable 698 cc
Model Q, which sold by the thousand.

1902 OLDSMOBILE
Launched in 1901, the
Curved Dash was the first
mass-produced car. At
Ransom E. Olds'
factory in the U.S.A.,
hundreds of parts were
made at once. These
were assembled in groups
(engine, chassis, body), and
then brought together to
complete the 4$\frac{1}{2}$-hp, 2-gear car.

HENRY FORD

In America, Henry Ford dreamed of building cars that everyone could afford. Improving on Olds' methods, he devised the assembly-line method of production. This enabled him to drop the price of his Model T from $850 in 1908 to $290 in 1925.

PUTTING AMERICA ON WHEELS

Ford's Model T was a massive success – more than 15 million rolled off the assembly line between 1908 and 1927. It had a simple chassis, which was robust enough to endure America's poor road surfaces. A pedal made gear-changing easy, while the 2.9-litre engine gave a top speed of 72 km/h (45 mph).

MODEL T ASSEMBLY LINE

Making cars on an assembly line meant that workers stayed in one place while the cars moved past them on a type of conveyor belt. As a result, the workers became fast at doing one specialized job. Here, bodies are dropped onto pre-built chassis moving down the line.

CARS FOR EVERYONE

THE FIRST CARS were too costly for most people, but the runaway success of Ford's Model T showed how cars could sell if they were cheap enough. In the 1920s and 1930s motoring became available to middle-class families, with cars such as the Austin 7 and Ford A. In 1939, Volkswagen and Citroën created ultra-cheap basic "people's" cars.

EARLY TRANSPORT
Motorbikes with sidecars were the cheapest transport for many families before small cars.

1920 CHEVROLET FB-4
Unlike the "490", the competitor for the Model T, the FB-4 was an upmarket car. With its elegant styling and the introduction of an electric starting motor, it made motoring easy.

1928 MODEL A FORD
The much-awaited successor to the Model T, the A was twice as powerful (40 hp) and a resounding success.

1928 AUSTIN 7
The "little Seven" was the first British car to sell in large numbers. It was small and light – 2.7 m (9 ft) long and under 500 kg (1,100 lbs) – and very cheap.

As handsome as you'll
meet anywhere

MORRIS OXFORD
SPORTS COUPÉS

SUCCESSFUL ADVERTISING

In the 1920s and 1930s, car makers appealed to middle-class families feeling the pressures of life in town. They posted adverts that emphasized how a car could make the countryside and the freedom of the open road available to a driver.

CAR FACTS

• The first British car to sell in millions was the Morris Minor 1000.

• Over 22 million VW Beetles have been sold.

• Over 35 million new cars are made each year.

1961 FIAT NUOVA 500

Until the 1960s, cheap cars were often used as utilitarian transport, with little need for style and comfort. Model Ts, 2CVs, and Fiat 500s were as likely to be seen carrying sheep on the farm as passengers on a shopping trip.

1986 CITROËN 2CV

Like the famous VW Beetle, the classic, ultra-basic Citroën 2CV was launched in 1939. It remained in production right up until the 1980s.

Sparse interior with canvas seats

Tiny but reliable low-maintenance engine

Simple, lightweight body

Suspension designed to carry a basket of eggs across a field without breaking

MASS PRODUCTION

ALTHOUGH HENRY FORD'S moving assembly line is still central to every car plant, he would be astonished to see today's factories. Instead of noisy workers, electronically controlled robots work silently, drilling, welding, and painting.

CEASELESSLY WORKING
Sparks fly as robots tirelessly weld floorpans and side panels into a stream of body-shells.

PAINT-BOX
Robots make ideal painters. They need no protection from harmful spray, and they are able to do a perfect job time after time.

GOOD PUPILS
Once a robot is "taught" a new job, like fitting this windscreen, it can do it over and over again.

Shells are rust-proofed before painting

Painted cars move to "oven" for drying

PRODUCTION FACTS

• American Edward Budd pioneered all-steel welded bodywork on Dodges in 1917.

• In 1992, Japan made 9.4 million cars.

• A typical family car contains around 14,000 separate parts.

Robot holds screen using strong suckers

A KIT OF MANY PARTS

Thousands of parts are pre-shaped before they come together on the assembly line. Complex units like the engine and electrical system are put together before they are installed. The suspension and wheels are put on last.

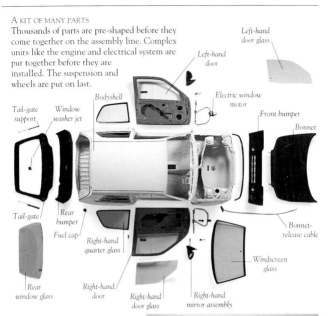

Left-hand door glass

Left-hand door

Electric window motor

Front bumper

Bonnet

Tail-gate support

Window washer jet

Bodyshell

Tail-gate

Rear bumper

Fuel cap

Right-hand quarter glass

Rear window glass

Right-hand door

Right-hand door glass

Right-hand mirror assembly

Bonnet-release cable

Windscreen glass

WELL STOCKED

Cars for export are taken to other countries on huge ships. Dealers order them through computer networks which organize the allocation. Sometimes, thousands of new cars are kept in huge storage compounds until they are needed for delivery.

CARS FOR EVERY OCCASION

THE NEW MOTOR INDUSTRY soon produced a variety of cars adapted for specific tasks, such as economy cars, luxury limousines, vans, sports cars, and family saloons. Only estate cars offered any real flexibility until the hatchback appeared in the 1960s. Today's spacious and speedy MPVs offer the best of all worlds.

THEN AND NOW

1930s
Fiat's tiny 570 cc Topolino ("Little Mouse") was the first car for many Italian families. Although slow, this attractive two-seater was cheap to run.

1990s
Hardly bigger than the Topolino, Fiat's Punto carries four people and is much faster. Its "two-box" hatchback form makes it very practical.

MULTI-PURPOSE VEHICLES (MPVS)
MPVs like this Renault Espace with its three rows of detachable seats and room for seven people are very versatile.

SALOON CARS
In the 1950s, the most popular type of car was the three-box saloon, with four or five seats and a separate boot. Today's cars are often sold as both saloon and hatchback models.

1958 FORD FAIRLANE SALOON

SPORTS CARS

The beautiful Jaguar XK120 of 1948 fits the classic idea of a sports car with its long bonnet, open top, and only two seats. There was a skimpy hood, but in this case, performance was more important than the comfort of the driver and any passengers. The XK120 also had a fair amount of boot space.

"One-box" shape

CAR FACTS

• Jaguar planned only a few XK120s, but actually built more than 10,000!

• Some cars were ahead of their time – in the late 1930s, Citroën were making a front-wheel-drive hatchback.

ESTATE CARS

Estate cars, or station wagons, were designed as utility vehicles. They had a large carrying space and the seats often folded down to give extra space. For many years, cars with timber-framed bodies and wood trim were fashionable. Today's estate cars are just as fast and as smooth as the saloon models.

1955 FORD SQUIRE ESTATE

1955

NATIONAL TYPES

MANY COUNTRIES have produced their own very distinctive types of car. Road size, fuel prices, the availability of spare parts, and traffic levels are all important factors. Other influences are the geography, history, and cultural life of the country.

BADGE OF SUCCESS
Fiat cars are synonymous with Italian life and culture. The Fiat company has been making cars since 1899.

HINDUSTAN AMBASSADOR
Introduced in 1957, India's Hindustan Ambassador is based on the old Morris Oxford. The car is easy to maintain in India, as parts can easily be made by the local blacksmiths.

Stylish fins typical of American cars of the 1950s

Finned hub cap

MICRO CAR

Parking space is at a premium in Japan's traffic-choked city streets, making compact micro cars such as Nissan's Be-1 highly popular. Narrow and short, they make parking easy, and enable the driver to qualify for low road taxes. Only a few thousand are made of each model, so they soon become collectors' items.

Tiny 660 cc engine

Bonnet space is for luggage; engine is in boot

Folding hood

VOLKSWAGEN BEETLE

The Beetle is the most famous German car ever produced. It was developed in Germany in the 1940s as a compact and affordable "people's car", and outlived its rivals to become the world's best-selling car.

CADILLAC COUPE DE VILLE

In 1950s America, petrol was cheap and cars were large, glamorous, and chrome-covered. This flamboyance expressed the wealth and hope of the post-war years. The sleek Coupé de Ville was ideal for long trips on the open road.

Wrap-around windscreen

Bonnet hides a smooth eight-cylinder engine

Protective rubber over-rider

Decorative white tyre ring

SELLING THE CAR

ONCE A COMPANY has spent millions developing a car, it must then spend even more bringing the new model to the market in order to sell it. Brochures, advertising campaigns, and television commercials must all be prepared, and cars delivered to every showroom; but the new shape must be kept secret until launch day. With luck, the new car will start to repay the cost after only three years – though many cars never do.

STILLS FROM
THE RENAULT
ADVERTISING
CAMPAIGN

STRETCHING THE TRUTH
In the 1950s, adverts often used drawings to make the product seem more attractive. This Buick gliding through the countryside has been "stretched" by the artist to look longer and lower than it is.

STARS OF THE SCREEN
Television is a powerful promotional medium. Cars are filmed in exotic locations, often in stories lasting only 40 seconds. Some storylines appear in successive adverts.

SECOND TIME AROUND
More second-hand cars are sold every
year than new cars. Used-car showrooms
are a familiar sight in most places.

HOW IT USED TO BE
With its Turkish carpets, oak panelling,
and vases of flowers, this smart 1930s
showroom provided a lavish background
for the sale of Talbots and Rolls-Royces.

TODAY'S SUPERMARKETS
Now, showrooms are less elaborate.
You can visit a "car supermarket",
with hundreds of cars under one roof.

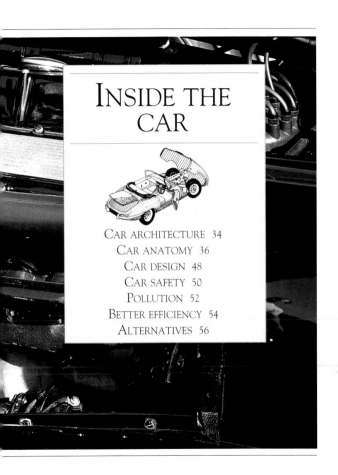

INSIDE THE CAR

CAR ARCHITECTURE

DESIGNERS HAVE always tried to pack as much as they can into as little space as possible. Early cars had a separate chassis with wood, fabric, or metal body panels built on. Today's steel-shelled, front-wheel-drive cars offer more strength and room, but weigh much less.

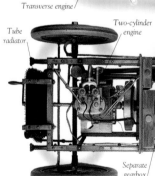

Radiator

Transverse engine

Tube radiator

Two-cylinder engine

1911 ROLLS-ROYCE SILVER GHOST
The huge chassis carried a timber frame, clad in metal. It was very high, to clear the drive shaft and rear axle. Despite the car's length, luggage went on the roof, and the driver had no weather protection.

Separate gearbox

1990S RENAULT CLIO
Made of thin steel panels, this car has front-wheel drive and small wheels that mean the driver and passengers sit close to the road. The strong shell allows for big doors, while remaining rigid.

1904 SYSTEME PANHARD CHASSIS
Most early cars had a Panhard layout, with the engine and gearbox aligned. Passengers sat above the rear axle.

NO SPACE WASTED

Designed around the passengers, the Seat Ibiza has its engine (in red) set across the car (transversely). The fuel tank is underneath the rear seat, and clever rear suspension leaves the boot free for luggage.

Hatchback opening

Exhaust

Silencer

1. FRONT ENGINE, REAR-WHEEL DRIVE

2. REAR ENGINE, REAR-WHEEL DRIVE

Drive shaft

Exhaust

3. FRONT ENGINE, FRONT-WHEEL DRIVE

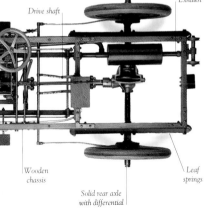

4. MID-ENGINE, REAR-WHEEL DRIVE

Wooden chassis

Leaf springs

Solid rear axle with differential

Engine position affects internal space, handling, and traction (road-grip). For years, layout **1** was the best compromise. Layout **2** is very good for grip but is poor on space. Most family cars use layout **3** for maximum space and good traction. Layout **4** gives fast sports cars good handling and grip, but little space.

CAR ANATOMY

A MODERN CAR usually has the engine at the front driving the front wheels, so leaving maximum space for luggage and passengers. The aerodynamic body, made from pressed steel, is welded into a single unit, with only the wings and doors separate.

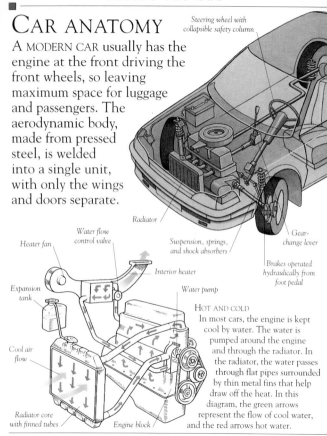

Steering wheel with collapsible safety column

Radiator

Heater fan

Water flow control valve

Suspension, springs, and shock absorbers

Gear-change lever

Interior heater

Brakes operated hydraulically from foot pedal

Expansion tank

Water pump

Cool air flow

Radiator core with finned tubes

Engine block

HOT AND COLD

In most cars, the engine is kept cool by water. The water is pumped around the engine and through the radiator. In the radiator, the water passes through flat pipes surrounded by thin metal fins that help draw off the heat. In this diagram, the green arrows represent the flow of cool water, and the red arrows hot water.

A MODERN CAR

A typical saloon car has the engine mounted transversely (cross-ways) to take up less space. The body panels are hollow with holes let into them to reduce weight, but the driver and passengers travel inside a very strong cage.

Exhaust pipe to carry away waste gases

Speedometer

Rev gauge

Fuel gauge

THE DASHBOARD

The word "dashboard" came from the wooden board that saved carriage-drivers being dashed by flying stones from horses' hooves. Today, dashboard displays show the car's speed, the fuel level, and so on.

MECHANICAL FUEL GAUGE 1930

Today, instruments are mostly electronic, but early ones were mechanical, like this fuel gauge. As the fuel went down, the float sank, and moved the needle.

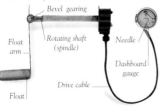

Bevel gearing

Float arm

Rotating shaft (spindle)

Needle

Dashboard gauge

Drive cable

Float

Trip distance recorder

Speed recorder

SPEED INDICATOR 1911

As the performance of the early cars improved, so more and more cars had speed indicators. This one not only showed current speed, but recorded the speed at points 50 yds apart over the previous 820 m (750 yds).

Under the bonnet

Some cars have the engine at the back. A
few sports cars have it in the middle. Most
cars have the engine in front under the
bonnet, together with most of the other
mechanical parts: the fuel system, the
electrical system (p. 42), the water cooling
system, and the gearbox and transmission
that link the engine to the wheels. The
battery, fuses, and the windscreen washer
bottle are also found under the bonnet.

KEEPING COOL
The Citroën 2CV (Deux
Chevaux) looks simple
under the bonnet because
its engine is cooled by the
flow of air, not an
elaborate water system.

INSIDE A CLASSIC
Modern cars look very different on the
outside, but they have much the same
kind of equipment under the bonnet as
this 1934 "baby" Austin Seven –
the first popular British car used
for family motoring in the 1930s.

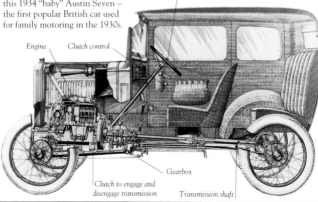

Horn

Engine   Clutch control

Gearbox

Clutch to engage and
disengage transmission

Transmission shaft

GEAR MOVEMENTS

LOW GEAR

HIGH GEAR

LOW AND HIGH GEARS

To start in low gear, a little cog on the input shaft meshes with a big one on the output, to turn the wheels slowly. In high gear, a big input cog meshes with a little output cog to spin the wheels fast.

REVERSE

GOING BACKWARDS

For reverse, a third gearwheel is slotted between the input and output to turn the output shaft the other way.

GEARED UP

The gearbox controls how fast the wheels turn compared to the engine speed or revs. By selecting the right gear, the driver keeps the engine at optimum revs at any speed.

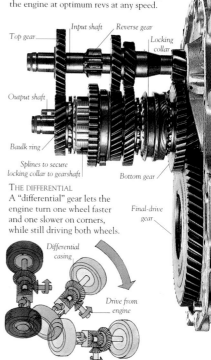

Input shaft   *Reverse gear*

Top gear   *Locking collar*

Output shaft

Baulk ring

Splines to secure locking collar to gearshaft

Bottom gear

THE DIFFERENTIAL

A "differential" gear lets the engine turn one wheel faster and one slower on corners, while still driving both wheels.

Final-drive gear

Differential casing

Drive from engine

Internal combustion

Most cars are driven by internal-combustion engines. Pistons in the engine harness the power released by exploding a mixture of fuel and air inside a number of cylinders. Petrol is the main fuel, but it is produced from oil, which is becoming increasingly scarce and expensive.

FUEL CONVERTER
Car engines change the energy stored in petrol into movement, releasing heat and exhaust gases.

Spark plug ignites fuel-air mixture

Phase 2: piston rises and squeezes fuel-air mixture

Valves open and close to admit and expel the fuel-air mixture

Phase 1: piston moves down and sucks in fuel-air mixture

Phase 3: mixture explodes, and expanding gases push piston down

Phase 4: piston rises, pushing waste gases out through exhaust valve

FOUR-STROKE CYCLE
Each cylinder takes turns at the four phases shown above. In a four-cylinder engine, one cylinder is always firing, giving smooth power. Water swirls round the pistons to cool them, and oil squirts onto all moving parts.

The crankshaft drives the wheels

Connecting rods change the pistons' up-and-down motion into the circular motion of the crankshaft

CYLINDER LAYOUTS

FLAT FOUR
A wide, low engine that gives good stability. Used by Subaru and, with six cylinders, by Porsche.

STRAIGHT FOUR
Efficient and compact – the most common layout. Two-, three-, and five-cylinder variations exist.

V-12
Expensive, super-smooth engine used in luxury saloons. Small sports cars use V-6s and V-8s.

TURBOPOWER
Turbochargers, driven by waste exhaust gases, force extra fuel-air mixture into the cylinders. This increases efficiency and power.

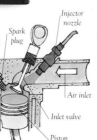

FUEL INJECTION
A fuel-injection system is much cleaner than a carburettor, and is essential with a catalytic converter. It uses a computer-controlled pump to squirt tiny, exact amounts of fuel into the engine.

CARBURETTOR
Fuel and air mix in the carburettor and are fed to the engine. As the piston descends, air whistles through the venturi and sucks fuel from the fuel bowl. Pressing the accelerator pedal opens the throttle valve, and allows more fuel-air mixture into the engine, increasing the speed.

The electrical system

A few cars run entirely on electricity; environmental demands may mean more all-electric cars will appear in the future. But even petrol-engined cars will not work without an electrical system to turn the engine, provide the spark to ignite the fuel, and power the lights, the windscreen wipers, and many other accessories. Many cars now also have electronically controlled functions, such as fuel injection.

Core

Insulator

SPARK PLUG
The tip of a spark plug is just a gap in an electrical circuit. But the voltage in this high-tension (HT) circuit is high enough – over 14,000 volts – to sizzle across the gap and provide the spark that ignites the fuel.

The coil boosts the 12-volt (low-tension - LT) current to over 14,000 volts for the spark

Battery to store current for starting

LT (12 -volt) supply

Distributor

HT leads

Headlamps

Distributor cap

HT lead from coil

Distributor body

HT plug leads

Key

Distributor rotor arm

A.E.I. unit

Spark plug

Sensor

Ignition switch

Electronic instruments

Alternator driven by the engine generates current and charges the battery

AUTOMATIC ELECTRONIC IGNITION
The distributor ensures the HT current goes to the right spark plug. Automatic electronic ignition (A.E.I.), found in many cars, ensures accurate spark timing.

LUCAS ACETYLENE
REAR LAMP

GAS LAMPS

Early car lamps ran on acetylene gas or oil. In this Lucas gas unit, the gas was made in the canister by water dripping on to carbide tablets. Electric lamps were not universal until the 1930s.

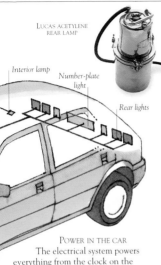

Interior lamp

Number-plate light

Rear lights

POWER IN THE CAR

The electrical system powers everything from the clock on the dashboard to the lights.

Negative terminal

Positive terminal

Lead negative plate

The plates sit in a bath of acid

Lead oxide positive plates

STORING POWER

All the car's electrical power comes from the alternator. It continuously charges the battery, which is able to store power for weeks by building up an electrical difference between two kinds of metal plates.

Condenser strengthens the spark

Vacuum advance provides earlier spark at high speeds

Spinning "rotor arm" briefly connects each plug in turn to the HT circuit

Points open to break the HT circuit and create a spark

DISTRIBUTOR

In older distributors, the timing of the spark was controlled by mechanical points. These were pushed open and shut by the four corners of a shaft turned by the engine.

Suspension and steering

A cart's wheels can simply rotate on rigid axles; a car's wheels must have suspension and steering too. Suspension isolates the wheels from the rest of the car with springs and dampers. So, when a wheel hits a bump, only the wheel moves up and down, not the whole car. This keeps the wheel in contact with the road and gives passengers a smoother ride. On most cars, the front wheels must swivel for steering.

Coil spring

Damper inside spring

SPRING AND DAMPER
When a wheel hits a bump, a coil spring absorbs the shock. A fluid-filled damper controls the bouncing of the spring.

CROSS SPRING
On the 1908 Model T Ford, there was only one spring for each axle, so the cars tended to roll and sway. On modern cars, each wheel is independently sprung.

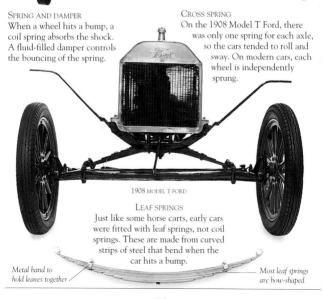

1908 MODEL T FORD

LEAF SPRINGS
Just like some horse carts, early cars were fitted with leaf springs, not coil springs. These are made from curved strips of steel that bend when the car hits a bump.

Metal band to hold leaves together

Most leaf springs are bow-shaped

WORM STEERING
Even very early cars
had a steering wheel
and a raked shaft. But
many had worm and nut
systems like this one. The
worm is the spiral thread on the end of
the shaft. As it turned, it moved
the sleeve-like nut up and down,
swivelling the wheels.

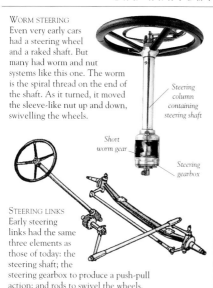

Steering
column
containing
steering shaft

Short
worm gear

Steering
gearbox

STEERING LINKS
Early steering
links had the same
three elements as
those of today: the
steering shaft; the
steering gearbox to produce a push-pull
action; and rods to swivel the wheels.

Link to
wheel

Rubber
protective gaiter

End of steering
shaft from wheel

Track rod

Swivelling "ball joint"

Pinion

Rack

RACK AND PINION
Most modern cars use rack and pinion steering. The
splined end of the steering shaft (the pinion) engages
with a row of teeth on the rack. As the shaft turns,
the rack is rolled left or right, swivelling the wheels.

FRONT SUSPENSION

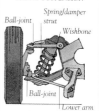

Ball-joint

Spring/damper
strut

Wishbone

Ball-joint

Lower arm

WISHBONE SUSPENSION
Wishbones are hinged
V-shaped arms with a
swivel joint at the apex.
They enable the steered
wheels to go up and
down as well as swivel.

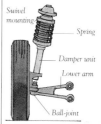

Swivel
mounting

Spring

Damper unit

Lower arm

Ball-joint

MACPHERSON STRUT
A swivelling coil and
damper unit called a
MacPherson Strut gives
lighter suspension for
front or rear wheels.

Wheels, tyres, brakes

The first cars jolted along on heavy wheels adapted from carts with wooden spoked wheels and solid rubber rims. Their brakes were either leather bands that squeezed hopefully on the axle, or rubber blocks like bicycle brakes. Today, cars have lightweight wheels made from pressed steel or alloy discs with pneumatic (air-filled) rubber tyres that give a soft ride and superb grip on the road. Hydraulic brakes give good braking power.

"BIBENDUM", TRADEMARK OF THE MICHELIN TYRE COMPANY

THE SANKEY WHEEL
Car wheels had pneumatic tyres as early as 1895, but punctures were frequent. So the arrival of the Sankey wheel in 1910 was a relief. It could be bolted on in seconds and the spokes were of light, hollow, pressed steel.

SANKEY WHEEL, 1910

LOCK-NUT, 1937
The wire wheels of 1930s Lagondas were held in place by a "knock-off" nut.

CROSS-SPOKES, 1913
Criss-crossing spokes meant light wire wheels could take braking forces.

JAGUAR E-TYPE, 1962
Sports cars had wire wheels for good looks and light weight into the 1960s.

CAST ALLOY, 1985
For sportier cars, wide aluminium and magnesium alloy wheels are popular.

CUSHION TYRE, 1903
Early pneumatic
tyres were narrow,
prone to puncture,
and so smooth that
they skidded badly
and slipped on hills
in the wet.

DISC AND DRUM BRAKES

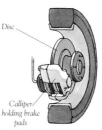
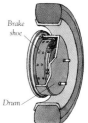

Disc

Calliper
holding brake
pads

Brake
shoe

Drum

DUNLOP 1909
By 1909, tyres
had angled
grooves for good
grip. They also
had inner tubes
pumped to high
pressure to keep
them on the
wheel rim.

DISC BRAKES
Most cars now have disc
brakes. These work by
using hydraulic pressure
to squeeze the steel disc
that is fixed to the wheel
between two pads.

DRUM BRAKES
The metal drum in old
drum brakes was fixed to
the wheel. Curved pads
or "shoes" pushed
against the inside of the
drum, slowing it down.

*Air-tight wheel rim means
no tube is needed*

*Tread channels water into grooves,
keeping rubber on road*

*Webbing helps
tyre keep its
shape*

TUBELESS
TYRE, 1947
Today, tubeless
low-pressure
tyres give good
grip and a
smooth ride.

MODERN TYRE
In wide, squat
modern tyres, an elaborate tread
disperses water and the rubber is
reinforced with a strong webbing of
nylon, rayon, and steel cords. In
radial-ply tyres, the cords run
radially out from the wheel's centre.

CAR DESIGN

MANY PEOPLE are needed to
design a new car. Designers
and engineers first establish
the shape and the running
gear. They then plan how to
build the car within a budget.
The car must look up-to-date,
despite the fact that the first
sketches may be three years old.

ON THE DRAWING-BOARD
Every car begins with a
drawing. Manufacturers
select the shapes they like,
then designers refine the
shapes to accommodate the
passengers and the
mechanical parts needed.

COMPUTER-AIDED DESIGN
The drawings are put onto a computer
screen. The three-dimensional images can
be altered to test the interior space,
strength, and weight of a design.

A "virtual reality"
car on screen

CLAY MODELS

A quarter-size model in smooth clay is sculpted to help the team decide on the final look. An accurate full-size model is made before the real car is manufactured.

QUARTER-SIZE MODEL OF WHOLE CAR

FULL-SIZE CLAY MODEL, OR "BUCK", OF INTERIOR

TUNNEL TESTING

Engineers check a car's aerodynamics in the blast from a wind-tunnel's huge propeller by using a pipe that emits a ribbon of smoke. They can change the angle of the car by moving it on a turntable.

OUT IN THE OPEN

Prototype cars are test-driven to destruction before production begins. To keep the new shape secret, new parts are sometimes fitted to old car bodies. Other vehicles are disguised with add-on panels to fool "spies" from motoring magazines.

CAR SAFETY

THERE ARE TWO KINDS of safety that should be practised on the roads. The first is active – good driver training, providing better road surfaces, and manufacturing manoeuvrable cars. The second, passive safety, is aimed at reducing injury if an accident does happen, with items such as seatbelts, crumple zones, and anti-skid brakes.

BULB HORN, 1911

EARLY WARNING
From the early days of motoring, horns have been used to warn of danger.

CRASH TEST
Engineers test new cars by deliberately crashing them into concrete blocks. Dummies inside carry sensors to see how passengers would fare, and slow-motion film is used to work out improvements.

Car "fired" along track into concrete block

AIRBAGS
In some cars, when a sensor feels an impact, it triggers a gas canister. This inflates a plastic balloon to cushion the face and chest.

Airbag deflates milliseconds after crash

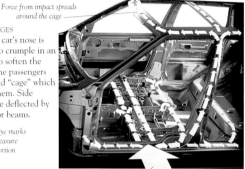

Force from impact spreads around the cage

SAFETY CAGES
A modern car's nose is designed to crumple in an accident to soften the impact. The passengers sit in a rigid "cage" which protects them. Side impacts are deflected by strong floor beams.

Bull's-eye marks to measure distortion

Side impact carried by floor beams

PROTECTING PASSENGERS
Wearing seatbelts saves lives, and using them is compulsory in most countries. Special seats can be fitted into cars to protect small children. Older children can sit on booster cushions and use the normal seatbelt.

POLLUTION

ENVIRONMENTAL DAMAGE from pollution is part of the price we pay for our cars. Disposing of old cars is also a huge problem, as some materials do not decompose. Cars are now designed so that as much material as possible can be recycled to save valuable resources.

CUBED CAR
After removing reusable material, old cars are crushed into small blocks by massive machines. The blocks are then melted for reuse.

Hard plastics are ground down and remoulded

Steel, plastic, glass, batteries, and radiator coolant are reprocessed

PLANNED REUSE
The coloured bits of this Mercedes are recycled parts from other cars. As much as 75 per cent of some cars can be reused, reclaimed, or reprocessed. Some items are "down-graded": bumpers are used for trim panels, upholstery for insulation, and brake fluid is turned into paint thinner.

CITY CAR DUMP

REGULATING EXHAUST EMISSIONS

Many countries now have regulations to control the pollution from car exhausts. Here, Thai technicians check that a van's exhaust does not break the law.

Face masks give limited protection from air-borne dirt and fumes

SMOG ALERT

In cities, pollution may gather and react with sunlight to produce "smog" – a thick blanket of harmful gas that lasts for days, and causes health problems. This traffic officer is wearing a protective mask.

POLLUTION FACTS

• The metal rhodium, used in catalysers, is so rare that every gramme must be recycled.

• In 1960, there were 125 million cars in the world; by 1994, there were 622 million.

TYRE MOUNTAIN

Getting rid of millions of old tyres is a world-wide problem. But scientists are now developing incinerators that can safely burn them for fuel.

Old tyres do not rot

When burned, old tyres produce dangerous gases

BETTER EFFICIENCY

CARS USE A HUGE proportion of the world's dwindling energy resources and are a major source of air pollution. Car makers are trying to make engines more efficient, with inventions such as electronic control. They are also trying to combat pollution by using catalytic converters and lead-free fuel.

ELECTRIC BMW
Many car makers are experimenting with electric cars, and some almost match petrol cars in performance. However, the power stations that supply the electricity also produce pollution.

EXPERIMENTAL
ELECTRIC
CAR

Engine cooled
with oil, not
water

Giant coil with thousands
of turns of wire

SOLAR FLAIR
The experimental Solar Flair gets all its power from 900 solar energy cells. These convert sunlight to electricity which drives the car.

ELECTRIC CAR ENGINE
Electric car engines get their power from batteries. These need recharging as often as a conventional car needs to top up with fuel. The problem is that recharging takes several hours.

Can reach 85
km/h (40 mph)

1896 BERSEY ELECTRIC CAB

Many of the very earliest cars ran on steam or electricity, not petrol. Indeed, electric carriages were very fashionable in the early part of the 20th century. But the improving performance and stamina of petrol engines soon left steam and electric cars standing.

Platinum on mesh helps convert carbon monoxide to carbon dioxide and steam

Rhodium on mesh helps convert nitrogen oxides to nitrogen and oxygen

CATALYTIC CONVERTER

Many new car exhausts are fitted with a converter. Inside is a mesh coated with platinum and rhodium, which act as catalysts to encourage a chemical reaction. This breaks down some of the pollutants in the exhaust to harmless gases and steam.

BP CHALLENGE

Fuel economy competitions have produced some odd-looking cars, and some astonishing results. The super-sleek BP Challenge covered over 10,720 km (6,700 miles) across Australia on 4.5 litres (1 gallon) of fuel!

SOLAR FLAIR

ALTERNATIVES

NO MATTER HOW much car engineers manage to reduce the fuel consumption of ordinary cars, the world's oil supplies are limited, and will one day run out. Also, accidents and traffic jams will continue until we reduce our use of the car. If drivers do not choose to use public transport for some journeys, then they may be forced to do so by laws and taxes.

STREETS FOR PEOPLE
This street in Amsterdam, Holland, is car-free. People walk and cycle, resulting in fewer accidents and less pollution. They use trams to travel across the city or to fringe car parks.

BICYCLES FIRST
Cycling is one of the cleanest and healthiest means of travel. Many town give bicycles priority, and special lanes and traffic lights protect cyclists from the dangers of motor traffic.

"BICYCLES FIRST"
TRAFFIC SIGNAL

THE REBIRTH OF THE RAILWAYS
New high-speed rail services, such as Japan's Bullet train, move hundreds of people using a fraction of the fuel that cars use, and may help to ease road congestion.

ENVIRONMENTALLY FRIENDLY BUSES
Buses and coaches must also clean up their act. Some cities already use electric buses. Tapping the large gas reserves under the oceans, this Norwegian bus runs on natural gas, which pollutes much less than petrol.

PAY AS YOU DRIVE
To dissuade people from driving cars, more charges may be made for using the roads, perhaps by toll booths like this one in the Austrian Alps.

LUXURY CARS

TRAVELLING IN STYLE

THE TECHNOLOGY and automatic assembly of recent cars would have astounded the early designers and craftsmen of great names such as Napier and Hispano. A fine car was a chance to show their skill. Coach-builders developed their own styles – some luxurious, some outrageous.

1914 SHEFFIELD SIMPLEX
Beautifully made and superbly flexible, these English cars proved too expensive to survive.

1925 HISPANO-SUIZA
The company was Spanish-French and had a brilliant Swiss designer called Marc Birkigt. Aperitif millionaire André Dubonnet built this amazing tulipwood body on an H6B to compete in the 1924 Targa Florio race.

BUGATTI
ROYALE 1931

CAR OF KINGS
Ettore Bugatti set out to build the finest car in the world with the enormous Royale. The 8-cylinder 13-litre machine had a staggering price-tag – £4,000 for the chassis alone! Six were built but only three were sold.

CONTINENTAL STYLE
Chosen by French high society for its
looks and performance, the
powerful Delage D8 had
beautiful bodywork, as
can be seen on this 1937
coupé. In the rare D8S
form, the car boasted 120 hp.
A rival to Hispano, Delage was
finally taken over by Delahaye.

*One-off hand-
built body*

AMERICAN CLASS
Packard offered the first
V-12 in 1915. By the
1930s, the Packard
Twelves had reached
new heights of
excellence and
elegance. They were
custom-built for rich clients.

*Aircraft techniques used
for building body*

*Unique
Packard grille*

NEWCOMERS
Typifying a new breed of quality
Japanese saloons, the V-8 powered
Lexus LS400 is fast, silent, and
dependable. It is also good value
compared to traditional
European luxury cars.

ENGINE POWER
Behind the stork
mascot was the Hispano-
Suiza's wonderful 8-litre
engine that brought sporting
successes and prestige.

BRITISH LUXURY

BRITAIN HAS A UNIQUE tradition of well-crafted luxury cars. This is partly because it is the home of the "best car in the world" – the Rolls-Royce. But Bentley, Daimler, Lagonda, and lost names like Lanchester, have all built worthy rivals.

Grille inspired by the Parthenon in Greece

R 1909

SPIRIT OF ECSTASY
The famous Rolls-Royce "Flying lady" dates from 1911. Today's version is smaller than the original and retracts into the radiator if it is hit.

The unmistakable profile of a Rolls-Royce

THAT FAMOUS GRILLE
Since the Silver Ghost of 1906, the shape of the Rolls-Royce radiator has been a well-guarded trademark.

LUXURY FACTS
• It takes three months to build a Silver Spirit.
• Rolls-Royce runs its own training school for chauffeurs.
• The British Royal Family has owned over 100 Daimlers.

INTERIOR ELEGANCE
This Rolls-Royce has all the comforts of a British luxury car, where quality is more important than fashion. The picnic tables are made from walnut, and the car is upholstered in the finest leather.

STABLEMATES

From 1919 onwards, Bentley Motors built fast, powerful cars. Although the firm was bought by Rolls-Royce in 1931, the cars still retained their distinctive character.

This R-type Continental of 1955 was streamlined to do 190 km/h (120 mph), and at the time was the most expensive car in the world.

THE BENTLEY WINGED BADGE STILL GRACES THE RADIATOR GRILLE

THE SILVER CLOUD

Most Rolls-Royces have carried the prefix "Silver". First sold in 1956, later Silver Clouds had the V-8 engine still used today.

DAIMLER OR JAGUAR?

Daimler, Britain's oldest car firm and once an offshoot of Daimler in Germany, merged with Jaguar in 1960. Today's 6-cylinder (above) and V-12 models exist in both Daimler and Jaguar versions.

SPIRIT OF SUCCESS

Rolls-Royces are famous for a smooth and silent ride. The Silver Spur is longer than the Silver Spirit, and for speed, there is a turbocharged Bentley version.

ROLLS-ROYCE
SILVER SPIRIT

GERMAN DE LUXE

THE GERMAN CAR industry dates back to 1885, and has a reputation for quality and high technical standards. In the inter-war years, when German cars were setting the racetracks alight, Mercedes-Benz and Horch set the standard. Today, Audi, BMW, and Mercedes-Benz maintain that position.

1927 MERCEDES-BENZ S
Designed by Ferdinand Porsche, the S became famous on the racetrack.

INSIDE THE MERCEDES 540K
This is the two-seater cabriolet version of the 540K, but it was also available as a four-seater and a seven-seater for state occasions, with armoured sides and bullet-proof glass.

1935 MERCEDES-BENZ 540K
The stunning Mercedes 540K sports tourer was one of the great cars of the inter-war years. When the driver floored the throttle, the supercharger powered the car to over 171 km/h (106 mph).

1931 HORCH V-12
The Horch V-12 was designed by Fritz Fiedler, famous for the BMW 328 sports car. With its well-crafted body and silky smooth engine, it was one of the classic luxury cars of the early 1930s.

MERCEDES-BENZ STAR
The company now called Mercedes-Benz, founded in 1885, is the oldest car maker. The company linked two motoring pioneers – Gottlieb Daimler and Karl Benz.

1994 AUDI A8
Audi pioneered four-wheel drive saloons with the Quattro. This high-tech, six-gear version has an all-aluminium body.

1994 MERCEDES-BENZ S500 COUPÉ
The 250 km/h (155 mph) Mercedes-Benz S500 is the pinnacle of German engineering. Among its many sophisticated features are double-glazed windows.

AMERICAN STYLE

THE 1930s WAS a golden era for American luxury cars. Famous marques such as Cadillac, Packard, Cord, and Pierce Arrow made vast, extravagantly styled cars for Hollywood stars to pose beside and Chicago gangsters to drive. Today, only Cadillac and Lincoln survive.

1931 CADILLAC V-16
The Cadillac's big 7.4-litre, V-16 engine – its 16 cylinders set in a V – was incredibly smooth. The car powered along at up to 160 km/h (100 mph).

1934 PACKARD V-12
The Packard Twelve of the 1930s was the ultimate in luxury. It was built only for the wealthiest clients. Its powerful engine ran almost silently.

1937 PIERCE ARROW V-12
The fabulously styled and very fast Pierce Arrow V-12 was almost custom-built for the rich. It came in three wheelbase lengths and 17 different body shapes.

1954 CADILLAC CONVERTIBLE
In the 1950s, Cadillac gave its cars prestige with dramatic styling and flashy chrome grilles and bumpers. The famous tailfins were inspired, according to designer Harley Earl, by the P-38 Lockheed Lightning fighter.

THE FAMOUS CADILLAC WING INSIGNIA

LINCOLN LUXURY
A great marque fallen on hard times, Lincoln was bought by Henry Ford in 1922. The company's reputation continued to grow with convertibles such as the Continental. Lincoln still ranks as one of America's premier makes.

A COMFORTABLE RIDE Limousine interiors are well-equipped – including a bar and a television!

1967 LINCOLN CONTINENTAL

ELDORADO
Produced from 1986 to 1991, this version of the Cadillac Eldorado had a V-8 engine. Less distinctive than the Eldorados that came before or after, the model only generated modest sales.

AMERICAN FACTS

• A Pierce Arrow V-12 was once driven 4,364 km (2,710 miles) across Bonneville Salt Flats in just 24 hours.

• The headlamps of the Cadillac V-16 swivel.

• Al Capone drove an armour-plated Cadillac.

EVERYDAY CARS

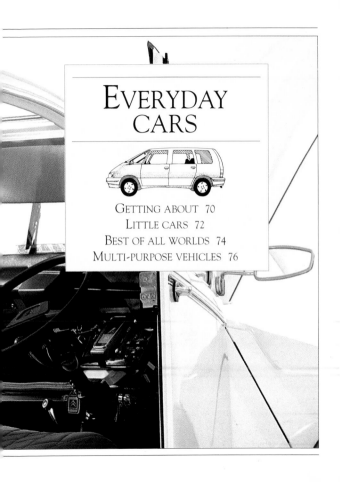

GETTING ABOUT

CARS SERVE MOST PEOPLE very well. They start in the coldest weather and need little routine attention. Any car today can do 130 km/h (80 mph), and many cars have electric windows and air-conditioning, whereas 30 years ago even heaters were an optional extra.

THE "PEOPLE'S CAR"
In 1959, East Germany produced a people's car called the Trabant. It had a 600 cc two-stroke engine, and the plastic body was reinforced with cloth.

SHOP WHEN YOU STOP
Every town has its automotive shop, where you can buy everything from spares to "goodies" such as fluffy dice.

DRIVER'S VIEW 1960
This 1960 Triumph Herald has only one instrument dial, a manual choke, and plastic seats. It has no heater, radio, safety belts, padding, or fresh-air vents.

DRIVER'S VIEW 1995
Luxurious by comparison, the Vauxhall Astra is still an ordinary family car. It has ergonomic controls, adjustable ventilation, and electric windows.

HANDS OFF
Fifty years ago, cars needed constant attention: owners had to grease joints, adjust brakes, change spark-plugs, and de-carbonize engines. Today, a car may be driven 10,000 km (6,250 miles) and only need the oil checked.

BEST FRIENDS
Many pets are experienced passengers. Detachable guards keep muddy paws off the seats, and pets can even wear safety harnesses.

WHEELS ON WHEELS
By fitting special racks, the family car can carry bulky leisure equipment such as sail-boards, skis, hang-gliders, or bikes.

LITTLE CARS

BY THE 1950s, cars were so easy to buy that city roads began to clog. As fuel became more expensive, demand grew for small, cheap cars. For a while, "bubble cars" were the rage, but it was the Mini, launched in 1959, that led the way, giving rise to today's compact cars.

MESSERSCHMITT
Like the Isetta, the Messerschmitt bubble car had a tiny, two-cylinder rear engine. The passenger sat behind the driver.

ISETTA BUBBLE CAR
The Isetta was conceived in Italy and developed by BMW in Germany, and had a tiny motor that drove the rear wheel. It was so short that it could fit into parking spaces endways. However, there was not much room inside, even for two people.

The new 3 wheeler ISETTA
the little miracle with a big heart
and a tiny thirst

AUSTIN MINI 1959
Mini designer Alec Issigonis created a full four-seater car in a tiny package. He did this by mounting the engine transversely to drive the front wheels. This set a precedent followed by all but a few small cars today.

FIAT 500
The rear-engined Fiat 500, launched in 1957, was even smaller than the Mini, and it was very popular in Italy, where the roll-back canvas roof made it great fun to drive in sunny weather. But the back seat allowed passengers little room.

FIAT CINQUECENTO
This is one of the classic small cars of the 1990s, with compact, front-engined, front-wheel drive. But its height gives passengers extra space.

TODAY'S COMPACTS
The Renault Twingo is typical of the modern breed of compact city cars. It is economic to run and its neat one-box shape can easily swallow four people and lots of gear. Its four wheels are set right at the corners for maximum passenger space and manoeuvrability.

INSIDE THE TWINGO
The Twingo's distinctive interior looks very different to most compacts, and is as plush as most bigger cars. There is only one equipment level and only one engine choice – style and simplicity are what matters.

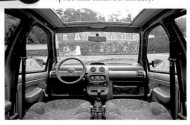

BEST OF ALL WORLDS

IT IS SURPRISING to think that the adaptable hatchback has only been popular for the last two of the motor-car's 11 decades. Pioneered by the Renault 16 in 1965, the hatch gained an asymmetrically split folding rear seat, so it could be a two-, three-, four-, or five-seater. Owners soon found other advantages – passengers could reach into the back on the move, and pets could be put in the rear.

PACKING CASES
Early cars, like this 1932 Daimler Double-Six, carried luggage in a separate trunk on the rear. Often the trunks were detachable, and could be carried inside for packing. But it was difficult to make them theft- and weatherproof.

UNDER COVER
By the 1940s, most saloons had a boot integrated into the body, like this 1948 Holden FX, Australia's first mass-produced car. Its construction meant there was room for a cavernous luggage compartment and accommodation for six people.

RENAULT LAGUNA RXE

MAXI-MINI
Although the Mini did have a boot, it was very small; those wanting more space could opt for the Traveller. Its extended wood-framed rear with double doors increased luggage capacity, but it remained an economical town car.

A QUESTION OF IMAGE
Although hatchbacks are practical, bigger executive cars like the Laguna are usually saloons. This is partly because it is harder to keep larger bodyshells rigid, but also because drivers often wish to avoid a "family" image.

DIFFERENT ENDINGS

THE HATCHBACK
Many mass-market cars offer a choice of body styles. Volkswagen's Golf is the base model from which the company developed the GTi.

THE ESTATE
For those needing more space, the same VW floorpan and mechanicals can be ordered with a full estate body, for use as a work or family car.

THE SALOON
For the traditional customer who prefers a separate boot, the Golf alters its name to the Vento. This is a relatively low-cost change.

MULTI-PURPOSE VEHICLES

SOMETIMES MORE SPACE is needed to carry extra people or cargo. In 1985, the Renault Espace started a trend towards the "one box", or multi-purpose vehicle (MPV). With its removable seats, the MPV can be a minibus, camper-van, family car, or mobile office; yet it is no longer than a hatchback and easy to drive.

ANCESTOR OF THE MPV
American William Stout launched his streamlined seven-seater Scarab in 1932. Only a couple were sold.

THE VW KOMBI
The first mass-produced MPV was Volkswagen's 1950s Kombi. With side doors and a rear engine, it was very adaptable, if slow and unwieldy. Many were built as motor-caravans, and the basic layout stayed the same until the 1980s.

Double doors for easy access

FIAT MULTIPLA
Not all MPVs are tall and square. In 1956, Fiat squeezed three rows of seats into its tiny 600 cc-engined Multipla. The result was a low, compact people-carrier that was well-suited to crowded Italian streets. It was popular as both a taxi and a family car.

High hatch doubles as a rain shelter

1990s FIAT ULYSSE

The Ulysse has a wind-cheating shape with sliding back doors. Air conditioning, power steering, an electric sun-roof, and a powerful engine make it a comfortable cruiser.

ULYSSE SEATING PLAN
The Ulysse's seats can be folded away, reversed, or taken out. Each seat has a built-in safety belt. The rear hatch is large so bulky cargo can be loaded.

MPV FACTS

• Between 1986 and 1994, MPV sales in Europe rose by 500%.

• A 1914 Alfa Romeo built by Italy's Count Ricotto was the first one-box shaped car.

MPVs IN THE U.S.A.
MPVs, or "minivans", such as Plymouth's Grand Voyager have largely replaced the traditional station wagon and the Recreational Vehicle (RV) – a large motor-home designed to drive on the wide American roads.

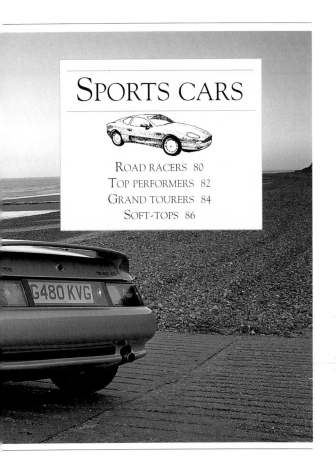

Sports Cars

ROAD RACERS

WHAT MAKES a sports car? The earliest "sportsters" were ordinary cars stripped down to the basics for maximum speed. Later, they were sleek tourers improved by such racing technology as the supercharger. Today, a sports car can be a 320 km/h (200 mph) monster or a stylish 660 cc "runabout".

ROAD RACER
Mercedes used a strong, light frame in the 300SL, making it ideal for racing. It won at Le Mans in 1952.

1957 MERCEDES-BENZ 300SL
The futuristic "Gullwing" could do 232 km/h (144 mph), but had little luggage space.

Gullwing doors
to clear high-sided frame

A 3-litre, 6-cylinder
fuel-injected engine

Engine tilted to
accommodate low bonnet

All-independent
suspension

Driving chain

Artillery wheels

No windscreen

CHAIN-DRIVEN 70HP MERCEDES
This was the car all wealthy drivers desired in 1904. Developed from the 60 hp racer, this 9.5-litre car could reach 137 km/h (85 mph) when stripped down like this. More luxurious versions carried a heavy touring body.

SPORTS CAR FACTS

• The first sports car was probably Vauxhall's 1910 Prince Henry.

• The world's most successful sports cars ever are Japan's Datsun 240/260/280 range.

• In 1953, Chevrolet's Corvette was the first mass-produced car with a fibreglass body.

• The first four-wheel-drive sports car was Jensen's 1966 FF.

AUBURN 851 SPEEDSTER
In 1935, designer Gordon Buehrig electrified America with this dramatic two-seater. With a supercharged eight-cylinder engine, each one was tested to 160 km/h (100 mph).

LE MANS
Since 1924, Le Mans has been the toughest of all sports car races. Cars pound the 13-km (8-mile) French track for 24 hours, changing drivers at refuelling stops.

SUZUKI CAPPUCINO
Today's small sports cars emphasize fun rather than speed. The Cappucino can only do 134 km/h (83 mph), but offers the thrill of classic open-road motoring.

Fold-away hard-top

Car has a 3-cylinder, turbocharged engine

TOP PERFORMERS

SOME CARS ARE BUILT to be driven very fast – above the legal limit in most countries. These supercars are the élite of the motoring world, drawing on racing technology for their sensational acceleration and superb handling. But the best is never cheap, and only the lucky few will ever drive one of these road rockets.

Butterfly doors stay open to see when reversing

BUGATTI EB110

BUGATTI EB110SS
The legendary Bugatti name of 1930s was revived for this supercar of the 1990s. It has a shattering top speed of 352 km/h (220 mph), and can go from 0 to 100 km/h (60 mph) in just 3.2 seconds.

HONDA NSX
Once nearly all the really fast cars were made in Europe, but in 1989 the Japanese company Honda built the NSX. With its stylish shape and speeds of more than 260km/h (165 mph), it is a match for its rivals.

LAMBORGHINI DIABLO

The stunning Lamborghini Diablo can accelerate away from standstill to over 160km/h (100 mph) in less than the time it takes you to read this sentence. It can then carry on to over 320 km/h (200 mph).

Aluminium and carbon-fibre construction

TOP PERFORMER FACTS

• A tuned version of the Chevrolet Corvette, the Callaway SledgeHammer, has been timed at 408 km/h (255 mph).

• The McLaren F1 goes from 0 to 160 km/h (100 mph) and back to 0 in less than 20 seconds.

JAGUAR XJ220

When it was launched in 1989, the XJ220 was the world's fastest production car. But on tests it "only" reached 340 km/h (213 mph) not 350 km/h (the 220 mph in its name).

MCLAREN F1

The McLaren F1 performs to match its astronomical pricetag of £634,500. Using racetrack experience, McLaren have created the world's fastest production car, with a top speed of 370 km/h (231 mph).

Driver sits in middle between two passengers

GRAND TOURERS

BACK IN THE 1920s, Grand Tourers were huge, open-top luxury cars that were used by wealthy people to cruise down to the south of France. However, in the 1950s this changed. Today's GTs are high performance hard-tops built for speed and style.

1954 LANCIA AURELIA
The Aurelia B20GT Coupé was the forerunner of the modern Grand Tourer. Its fastback styling was designed by Pininfarina, and it had a powerful 2.5-litre V-6 engine, and a top speed of 177 km/h (111 mph).

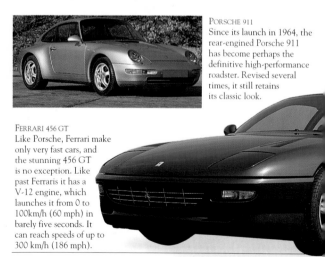

PORSCHE 911
Since its launch in 1964, the rear-engined Porsche 911 has become perhaps the definitive high-performance roadster. Revised several times, it still retains its classic look.

FERRARI 456 GT
Like Porsche, Ferrari make only very fast cars, and the stunning 456 GT is no exception. Like past Ferraris it has a V-12 engine, which launches it from 0 to 100km/h (60 mph) in barely five seconds. It can reach speeds of up to 300 km/h (186 mph).

ASTON MARTIN DB7

Aston Martin's DB5 was the most famous of all GTs in the 1960s, when it was driven by film spy James Bond. This is its 1990s successor.

BENTLEY CONTINENTAL R

Costing over £180,000, the Continental is a large Grand Tourer in the old style. It is fabulously luxurious, but surprisingly fast, and carries five people comfortably at over 230km/h (130 mph).

VAUXHALL TIGRA

Grand tourers need not be expensive – Vauxhall used the Corsa's simple running gear to create the speedy, stylish, and inexpensive Tigra coupé.

SOFT-TOPS

FOR SHEER DRIVING fun, there is nothing to beat an open-top sports car. The heyday of the "soft-top" was the 1950s with such classics as the Austin Healey 3000 and the Mercedes 300SL. Lately, convertibles have become popular again and appear in all the big manufacturers' catalogues.

1958 CHEVROLET CORVETTE
Designed by the legendary Harley Earl to rival the XK120, the Corvette was long known as "America's only sports car". It was immortalized in the song "Little Red Corvette".

Detachable roof panel

Lightweight fibreglass body on steel tube chassis

CATERHAM 7

Designed by Lotus' legendary Colin Chapman in the 1960s, the Caterham makes absolutely no concessions to comfort. It has two hard seats and a powerful engine, and serious drivers love it.

ALFA ROMEO SPIDER

Alfa Romeo's Spider was one of the classic sports cars of the 1960s. When this new V-6 Spider was launched in 1995, it too was hailed as a classic for its style, its 208-km/h (130-mph) performance, and its superb handling.

FIAT PUNTO CABRIO

Not all soft-tops are two-seater sports cars. Many small four-seater saloons such as Fiat's Punto are now given a tuned-up engine and hood to create a practical but fun convertible.

A 5-litre, fuel-injected V-8 engine

TVR GRIFFITH

TVR began in the 1950s, making cars in kit-form. Now, the company is one of the U.K.'s leading sports car makers. The Griffith is very noisy and very fast, roaring up to 96 km/h (60 mph) in barely four seconds. It is capable of speeds over 260 km/h (165 mph).

SPORTS CAR FACTS

- Ferrari's "prancing horse" badge recalls a First World War pilot.

- The term convertible dates back to 1904 and the Thomas Flyer.

- 94% of classic MGA sports cars of the 1950s were exported.

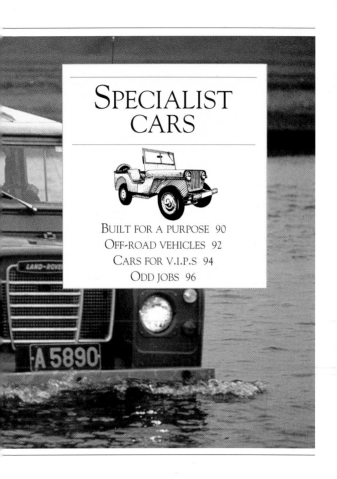

SPECIALIST CARS

BUILT FOR A PURPOSE 90

OFF-ROAD VEHICLES 92

CARS FOR V.I.P.S 94

ODD JOBS 96

BUILT FOR A PURPOSE

CARS CAN BE specially adapted to
do a variety of unusual jobs. Some,
such as 4x4 ambulances and fire-
engines, provide rescue services
over difficult ground. Some carry
specialized equipment for first aid,
broadcasting, or breakdown repair.
Others house signalling equipment,
loudspeakers, or fittings to move
special cargoes. The jobs are
limited only by the imagination.

ON THE GREEN
The golf buggy is perhaps
the most familiar electric
vehicle around. It is well-
suited to its task, with
wide, soft tyres to prevent
damage to the greens.

OUTSIDE BROADCAST
This BBC Land-Rover is
packed with electronics
and carries a telescopic
aerial to broadcast.

STREET STUDIO
So interviews can be
conducted inside and
"live" on air, this radio
car is sound-proofed.

VW CARAVELLE
RADIO CAR

GRANDSTAND VIEW
This off-road vehicle is equipped with platforms for tourists to see wildlife on the Masai Mara, Africa.

EYE-CATCHER
Some police cars have no markings to trap dangerous drivers. Others, like these French vehicles, have reflective stripes and message systems.

BLUES AND TWOS
Blue flashing lights and a two-tone siren, as on these Ladas in Moscow, are common signs of police cars.

OFF-ROAD VEHICLES

CONVENTIONAL CARS quickly get
stuck if they stray off the road. To
drive on mud, rock, snow, sand,
or other rough surfaces, cars need
tough construction, high ground
clearance, and four-wheel drive.
The first off-road cars, the Land-
Rover and the Jeep, were basic,
but today's off-roaders have all the
comforts of conventional cars.

1940 WILLYS JEEP
The passion for cross-
country driving began
after the Second World
War, when the U.S.
Army sold off used Jeeps.

SUZUKI VITARA
The two-litre Vitara V-6 is
typical of many current off-
roaders. It has four-wheel
drive for occasional off-road
use, but also gives fast and
comfortable travel on
ordinary roads where it is used
most of the time.

CHEROKEE JEEP
This Cherokee has all the
classic off-road features –
four-wheel drive, high
ground clearance, and a
short nose and tail. A
powerful 4-litre engine
and low gears mean that
it is especially good for
climbing steep banks.

RANGE ROVER

The Range Rover was the first four-wheel drive vehicle to handle as well on the road as off. It makes an excellent police car, and copes with different surfaces – for example, the smooth tarmac of a motorway and the rough earth of a ploughed field – equally well.

LAND-ROVERS HAVE EXTRAORDINARY CLIMBING ABILITY

LAND-ROVER

Functional, reliable, and phenomenally tough, the Land-Rover is the classic off-road vehicle. Introduced at the end of the 1940s, and still in production 50 years later, it is sold in nearly every corner of the world.

High air intake for driving through water

CARS FOR V.I.P.s

MOST PEOPLE HAVE to make do with basic
mass-produced cars, but famous people
often have custom-built cars. The cars
may be enlarged to provide room for
an entourage, made higher to allow others to see
V.I.P.s at public events, armour-plated for protection
from assassins, or simply made more luxurious.

THE POPEMOBILE
When his Holiness the Pope travels
abroad he sometimes rides in a high-
visibility vehicle, fitted with
armoured glass.

A CAR FOR THE QUEEN
Queen Elizabeth II and other members
of the royal family often travel to and
from state occasions in a
custom-built Rolls-Royce
Phantom VI. Deep
windows allow the
Queen to be seen as
she waves to the
crowds.

*Flying Lady is
replaced by silver
St George mascot
on state occasions*

ROW 813M

POP STAR OR OIL MAGNATE?
A specially elongated car like this Cadillac "stretch" limousine is ostentatious and gives plenty of room for guests in the rear compartment. Dark, smoked glass keeps the identity of passengers a mystery to bystanders.

PROTECTING A PRESIDENT
Attempted assassinations have forced American presidents to be very wary when travelling by car. Not only do they have armed guards, like those in this film still, but the presidential Lincoln is armour-plated with steel 4 cms ($1^1/2$ ins) thick, and the glass will stop high-velocity bullets.

GETTING MARRIED
Everyone is a V.I.P. on at least one special day. Rolls-Royces are popular for weddings, but many couples hire classic vintage cars such as this 1920s Austin Twelve.

Hand-built body takes months to finish

There are five Phantoms in the royal fleet

ODD JOBS

MOST EVERYDAY CARS are mass-produced in their thousands or millions. Others are custom-built or adapted for particular tasks. Some of these one-offs are simply for show, such as the car built in the shape of a swan in 1910 for a Scots millionaire. However, many of them are highly practical, and built for specific functions.

Raised platform gives unimpeded view

Stabilizing legs stop platform tipping

CAMERA PLATFORM
By adding a hydraulic lifting platform, a Land-Rover pick-up has been transformed into a mobile camera that can be moved anywhere.

MOVING SHOTS
This electric TV platform is perfect for tracking moving subjects, such as runners or racing cyclists. It is compact and gives an all-round view.

INVALID CAR
This electric car can carry a disabled person as close as possible to their destination. The seat swivels and there are no foot controls; all the controls are on the tiller.

Small wheels for manoeuvrability

RESCUE VAN
This AA (Automobile Association) rescue van is a mobile garage, adapted from an ordinary van to make roadside repairs as simple as possible. The tailgate lifts for access to equipment.

THE JEEPNEY
In the Philippines, unmade roads turn to quagmires after the torrential monsoon rains. Instead of buses or taxis, the locals use specially adapted jeeps, or "Jeepneys".

Bonnet adorned with polished ornaments

Bright paintwork to driver's design

Bus body hand-built from wood for minimum cost

Chrome hubcaps give the functional wheels a touch of glamour

Four-wheel drive

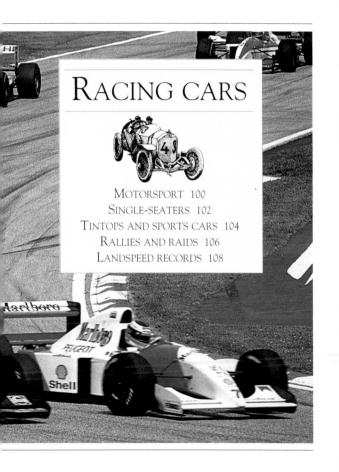

RACING CARS

MOTORSPORT

THIS IS AN EXCITING sport, but expensive and sometimes risky. For drivers, it demands skill and nerve; for teams, it offers glory; for sponsors, it provides invaluable advertising; for manufacturers, there are vital technical lessons. Televised races draw huge sponsorship, but people also race in less glamorous events.

SPARE TYRES
Competitors fitted twin wheels to improve the grip of narrow tyres in the 1950s.

POWERHOUSE
The V-10 Renault RS10 engine which powers Formula One cars has over 700 bhp. It needs to be rebuilt every 480 km (300 miles).

Engine revs to 14,000 rpm

Fuel-injection intakes

Quadruple camshafts

Load-bearing alloy block

Five-into-one exhausts

THEY'RE OFF
Hearts pound at the first corner of the Canadian Grand Prix. This is the riskiest moment of the dramatic two-hour battle seen by millions on television. Winners must be dedicated and superbly skilled.

Net to catch debris

Full-face helmet with air-supply

Fireproof bib to protect neck

SAFETY FIRST
Racing is actually quite a safe sport. All drivers wear flameproof clothing and helmets. Cars must have safety harnesses, strong roll-cages, and built-in fire extinguishers.

Fireproof gloves

WIN SOME, SELL SOME
Touring-car races feature saloons which resemble popular road cars. Here, an Alfa Romeo 155 leads the pack. In fact, these cars are so highly tuned that you could never drive one on the road. But they provide exciting close racing.

SECOND TIME AROUND
This Maserati 250F, and the Cooper-Bristol behind, are 40 years old – and still racing.

Bristol engine developed from pre-war BMW

SINGLE-SEATERS

THESE CARS ARE pure racers – noisy, cramped, and very uncomfortable. The driver squeezes into a tiny cockpit, and perches on a thin strip of foam plastic. Thousands of newcomers enter junior series, using simple small-engined machines, but only a few make it to Formula One, with its powerful state-of-the-art technology.

READY FOR PAINTING
This Formula Three car has complex moulded carbon-fibre panels.

FORMULA ONE
The World Championship for Drivers is run to Formula One rules. These high-tech machines are staggeringly fast round corners, the tyre grip helped by the downforce from the wings.

Air intake with roll hoop

AT THE WHEEL
F1 engines are so noisy that the team manager has to plug in an intercom to speak to the driver when they discuss performance and lap times. Planning the best strategy at pitstops is as important as driving skill.

MONACO

Worldwide television coverage and sponsorship make Formula One a multi-million dollar business. This is why Monte Carlo comes to a halt every May for the famous Grand Prix (GP). The profit from hosting a GP is enormous.

PACIFIC
FORD PR02

*Multiple wing
for downforce*

*Streamlined
suspension arms*

*Radiators
hidden in
side-pods*

INDIANAPOLIS

America's top series peaks at the huge banked oval of the Indianapolis track. Numbers on the tower help the crowd keep track as the leaders speed through.

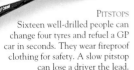

PITSTOPS

Sixteen well-drilled people can change four tyres and refuel a GP car in seconds. They wear fireproof clothing for safety. A slow pitstop can lose a driver the lead.

TINTOPS AND SPORTS CARS

RACING IS DIVIDED into many types or "formulae", so that the drivers can compete on equal terms. The very earliest racers were really sports cars carrying a mechanic as well as the driver. Even now, there must be room for a second seat for a sports car to qualify. Today, the toughest racing is among saloon cars, but smaller and cheaper cars can also compete.

TRACK STAR
Few manufacturers have been as successful as Mercedes-Benz. This 1952 300SLR had a straight-eight fuel-injected engine with "desmodromic" (springless) valves.

TERRIBLE TWINS
It is not outright speed that counts in a good race. These stripped Citroëns still use their two-cylinder motors, which means cheap sport, but it is the skill of the drivers that makes the race exciting.

SPECTATOR SPORT
Huge crowds used to line the roads during the Mille Miglia, the 1,600-km (1,000-mile) sports car race around Italy. Cars started at one-minute intervals. This Ferrari is crossing the finishing line in Brescia in 1952, after hours of full-throttle motoring.

NIGHT AND DAY
From the 1970s on, racing sports cars became radically different from anything in the showroom. These 1980s cars at Le Mans could never be used on the road. More recently the rules have changed to encourage grand tourers from Jaguar, Venturi, Lotus, and Chevrolet.

RACE-BRED
If the rules forbid adding "extras" for racing, then those extras have to be made standard in the showroom. Porsche's famous "whale-tail" spoiler was designed for the track, but had to be available for road cars too.

Huge spoiler cuts aerodynamic lift at speed

RALLIES AND RAIDS

RALLYING IS ONE of the toughest of
all motor sports. Each car is timed
individually at control points over
up to 40 stages. The rally makes
phenomenal demands on both cars
and drivers as they roar at speed
through anything from howling
blizzards to deep mud. The adapted
cars are based on saloon cars.

LIGHT ARRAY
Rally cars have extra
high-power spotlights and
foglamps in order to cope
with night stages and fog.

PARIS-DAKAR RALLY 1991
The toughest rallies are the desert
"raids", and the most famous is
the Paris–Dakar. The
upgraded suspension
on rally-raid cars
carries them
over desert
rocks.

ON COURSE
Every rally driver has to
have a co-driver, not only
to show the way but also
to give "pace-notes" to
indicate how fast to drive
on a particular stretch.

SMALL WONDER
The Mini made a huge impact in 1960s
rallies, beating bigger and more powerful
cars. It is still winning in historic rallies.

4X4 FORD
To travel fast on the roughest roads in
all conditions, top rally cars have very
tough suspension and four-wheel drive.

FORD COSWORTH ON ACROPOLIS RALLY

Bucket seat for
extra support

Emergency engine
hill-switch

Timers to check pace
on each section

COSWORTH INTERIOR
Rally cars look very
different on the inside
from street cars. Gone are
the carpets and rear seats.
Driver and co-driver sit
in lightweight "bucket"
seats inside a tough steel
roll-cage to protect the
crew if the car overturns.

LANDSPEED RECORDS

ONLY A FEW YEARS after Benz built the *Motorwagen*, drivers began competing to be the fastest on earth. As speeds spiralled upwards, the cars moved from roads to salt flats or deserts to provide the minimum necessary 20.8-km (13-mile) course. Since 1964, all new records have been set by jet-engined cars.

Body shaped over huge, treadless tyres

Tall fin for high-speed stability

1899 LA JAMAIS CONTENTE
Belgian Camille Jenatzy's electric "torpedo" took him to 105.85 km/h (65.79 mph) in 1899, Jenatzy went on to become a great racing driver.

1929 GOLDEN ARROW
Powered by a big aircraft engine, the Golden Arrow propelled Henry Segrave along Daytona Beach at 372.39 km/h (231.44 mph). This was the beginning of a decade of frantic record-breaking, during which Sir Malcolm Campbell first used Bonneville Salt Flats, the scene of most attempts since.

Bluebird over 9 m (29 ft) long

THE BLUE FLAME
Gary Gabelich used a rocket motor to power Blue Flame to 995.85 km/h (622.41 mph) across the salt flats at Bonneville in 1970.

THE BLUEBIRDS
Malcolm Campbell and his son Donald kept the name Bluebird for all their record-breaking cars and boats. This one, the last, used a gas-turbine aircraft engine and carried Donald to 648.59 km/h (403.10 mph) in 1964.

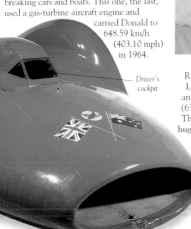

Driver's cockpit

WHO'S NEXT?
Richard Noble has now held the Land Speed Record longer than anyone else. He did 1019.24 km/h (633.46 mph) in Thrust 2 in 1983. Thrust 3, shown here, will use two huge jet engines to give it the power it needs to surpass Mach 1.

Large air-intake to feed gas-turbine

SPEED FACTS
• Thrust 2 used solid titanium wheels to skate over the desert.

• There is a separate class for wheel-driven machines.

• A record speed is an average of one run each way over a measured mile in an hour.

CLASSIC CARS

CLASSICS THROUGH HISTORY

WHAT IS A CLASSIC CAR? To some, it is anything over 20 years old; to others, it is a car that is rare and beautiful. The greatest cars are obvious candidates, but some surprisingly ordinary machines remain popular long after they cease production. There are clubs for Model T Fords, Minis, and Fiat 500s, and supplying parts is big business.

AUSTIN A35
Built as a basic small car, the 1956 Austin A35 was not a revolutionary vehicle. Fitted with a 34 bhp 948 cc engine, it could only reach 115 km/h (72 mph). But it is popular today, and many are tuned for racing.

Four exhaust pipes and silencers

Five-spoke alloy wheels

MG MIDGET
Independent suspension and disc brakes on the front of the 1961 Midget made the most of an economical 1300 cc engine. Parts and services are available so it is one of the cheaper sporting classics.

PORSCHE 959

This technically superb car was a significant engineering advance and so qualifies as a classic. It also won several major rallies. Its sophisticated electronics controlled the engine power and drive to all four wheels. Though extremely costly, much of the technology has now filtered down to "affordable" Porsches. A total of 259 were built of this model.

Cabin trimmed in leather and chrome

FERRARI DAYTONA

The 1973 Daytona is very rare. It has Ferrari's 4.4-litre V-12 engine, does 278 km/h (174 mph), and has won races. It is a classic on every count.

Quad pop-up headlamps

CLUE TO THE FUTURE

In 1994, Bentley unveiled the Java concept car at the Geneva Motor Show. If it is produced, it may herald a new line of smaller-engined classic Bentleys.

Concept Java

CLASSIC FACTS

• At a 1990 auction, a 1963 Ferrari GTO was bought for £6,350,000.

• The oldest motoring organization is the Automobile Club de France, founded in 1893.

VINTAGE GREATS

THE TERM "VINTAGE CAR" is often used instead of "old car", but it really refers to cars that were acknowledged as superb in their time and are still prized today by collectors. These fine and rare cars from particular periods are usually expensive, but their real value to an enthusiast is in their beauty, craftmanship, and speed.

PRESTIGE ORIGINS
Delage was one of France's premier pre-war makes. Its successful early racers, like this 1911 3-litre, carried a reputation for quality.

Supercharger in front of grille

1930 BENTLEY
W. O. Bentley's big, tough, fast cars won Le Mans five times up to 1930. Many of these magnificent machines still race today.

1930 SUPERCHARGED 4.5-LITRE BENTLEY

GY 3905

SIMPLE AND SPEEDY
MG began by tuning Morris tourers, but
soon produced the first cheap, simple
British sports car, the 1929 M-type
Midget. Later, they developed
rapid racers, like this rare
supercharged J-type of 1931.
However, MG continued to
offer low-cost fun motoring,
right up to the MG-F of today.

*Aero-screens instead
of windscreen*

"Fishtail" exhaust

DUESENBERG SJ
Perhaps the finest American
cars ever built, the
Model J Duesenbergs
were beautifully put
together. And the
supercharged SJ
(320 bhp), which
can do 206 km/h
(129 mph) is the
most desirable of all.

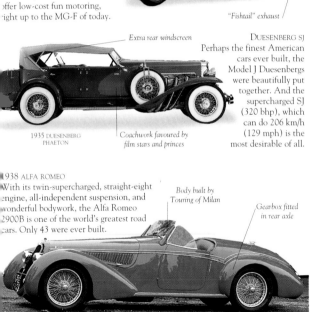

Extra rear windscreen

1935 DUESENBERG
PHAETON

*Coachwork favoured by
film stars and princes*

1938 ALFA ROMEO
With its twin-supercharged, straight-eight
engine, all-independent suspension, and
wonderful bodywork, the Alfa Romeo
2900B is one of the world's greatest road
cars. Only 43 were ever built.

*Body built by
Touring of Milan*

*Gearbox fitted
in rear axle*

VINTAGE RACING

LOOKING AT AN OLD racing car, it is hard to remember that it was once at the leading edge of technology. Many were scrapped after only a year to make way for an improved model. Others found a new life in vintage racing. Today, the oldsters are as fast as ever, and expertly maintained by their drivers.

IN THE PADDOCK
In the 1920s, when motor racing was the hobby of the rich, Brooklands was the home of huge aero-engined racers built to roar around the banking.

Engine behind driver

Small, light chassis

BACK TO FRONT
Cooper brought about a revolution by winning with rear-engined cars. Here, Maurice Trintignant races at Monaco in 1959. Today, these machines compete in historic racing events.

PIONEER DAYS
This scene in the 1906 Vanderbilt Cup in the U.S.A. is something you cannot see recreated today. Although many Edwardian models still race, there is no modern-day equivalent of these open-road races.

Mechanic ready to change tyres

UPHILL WORK

This M-type MG coupé is tackling a loose-surfaced climb during trials in 1932. Hill trials are still popular in Britain. Cars new and old slither up muddy slopes that put 70-year-old vehicles on an equal footing with modern machinery.

ALL-TIME GREAT

Alfa Romeo's P3 was the first single-seater Grand Prix car; it dominated the sport in the 1930s. Despite their rarity, they still race roday.

THE GOOD OLD DAYS

Take away the helmets and crash barriers, and the scene below could be from the 1930s. Instead, these Bugattis and Alfa Romeos at Cadwell Park circuit in England are 60 years old. They simply never stopped racing.

POST-WAR GREATS

IT TOOK THE CAR industry several years to bring new products out after the end of the Second World War. Basic transport was a first priority, but gradually new sports and luxury machines appeared. Their styling reflected the new era, and new technology arrived with the resumption of motor-racing. The 1950s produced significant machines, some destined to become classics.

MERCEDES 300SL
Despite tremendous war damage, Mercedes was able in 1952 to produce a top-level racing car, with advanced engineering and a 215 bhp engine. They are expensive rarities today.

TRIUMPH TR2
Triumph's 1953 two-seater reached 160 km/h (100 mph), despite its humble running-gear. Sturdy and simple, it won many rallies, and is a popular choice for historic rallying today.

Wind-cheating tapered tail

CHEVROLET CORVETTE
When General Motors needed a show-stopper in 1953, they built the striking Corvette in fibreglass. Its success made it a legend, and through many evolutions, it has retained its shape. Early 'Vettes are favourite American sports cars.

VW KARMANN-GHIA
A stylish body can disguise mundane mechanicals. Italian coach-builders Ghia re-clothed the Beetle in 1955, and the resulting Karmann-Ghia was a huge success. Convertibles (1957-1965) have become especially collectible.

BENTLEY CONTINENTAL
By fitting a streamlined body to the R-type chassis in 1953, Bentley produced the world's fastest four-seater. It did 192 km/h (120 mph) in silky silence – at a huge price! Only 208 were made, but many survive.

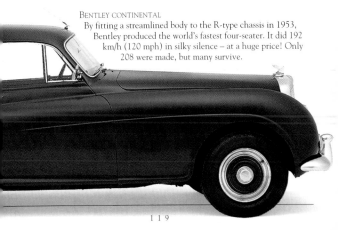

The 1960s

The decade of the 1960s saw the look of cars change dramatically. For the first time, some cars were made not with a separate chassis and body, but as a single unit. The square look that had dominated cars since the early days gradually gave way to a more rounded, curvy shape. At the same time, road cars were getting so fast that aerodynamic styling began to be crucial, and cars became low and sleek.

FORD MUSTANG
Ford's "pony" cars of 1964 set a trend for fastback saloons, appealing to those with a wild streak.

LAMBORGHINI MIURA
The 275-km/h (172-mph) Miura was the first modern "supercar" and caused a sensation when it was unveiled at the 1966 Geneva Motor Show. Many others have adopted the same transverse, mid-engine position.

A 6-cylinder, 4-litre engine under bonnet

ASTON MARTIN DB5
The Aston Martin DB5 was the classic British GT of the 1960s. The car was launched as the DB4 in 1958 with a platform chassis and a body by Italian GT coach-builders, Touring. The car went through various versions before being discontinued in 1970.

Aston's trademark grille

Wire wheels

1037 TE

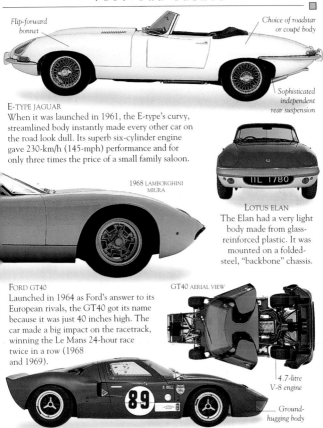

Flip-forward
bonnet

Choice of roadstar
or coupé body

Sophisticated
independent
rear suspension

E-TYPE JAGUAR
When it was launched in 1961, the E-type's curvy,
streamlined body instantly made every other car on
the road look dull. Its superb six-cylinder engine
gave 230-km/h (145-mph) performance and for
only three times the price of a small family saloon.

1968 LAMBORGHINI
MIURA

LOTUS ELAN
The Elan had a very light
body made from glass-
reinforced plastic. It was
mounted on a folded-
steel, "backbone" chassis.

FORD GT40
Launched in 1964 as Ford's answer to its
European rivals, the GT40 got its name
because it was just 40 inches high. The
car made a big impact on the racetrack,
winning the Le Mans 24-hour race
twice in a row (1968
and 1969).

GT40 AERIAL VIEW

4.7-litre
V-8 engine

Ground-
hugging body

The 1970s

Gullwing doors

In the early 1970s, manufacturers were still making cars that had few environmental constraints or safety features and little fuel economy – the biggest Ford Thunderbird dates from this time. Then the energy crisis caused makers to look at fuel economy and to clean up exhaust systems. At the same time, new U.S. safety regulations forced changes in body design.

CITROËN SM

SUSPENSION UP
Citroën's SM had a suspension system based not on metal springs but on fluid and gas.

SUSPENSION DOWN
An engine-driven pump raised or lowered the suspension, or changed its stiffness to suit the load.

DELOREAN
The DeLorean sports car was the brainchild of American car mogul John DeLorean. The car was developed in Belfast, Northern Ireland, with millions of pounds of U.K. government backing. The company collapsed within a few years of the launch.

FERRARI BOXER BB512
The Boxer was the 1970s classic supercar. The 4.4-litre flat-12 engine was called a "boxer" because its cylinder banks were in two horizontally opposed rows.

INTERIOR OF BOXER

Distinctive brushed steel bodywork

PRV V-6 engine developed by Peugeot, Renault, and Volvo

PONTIAC FIREBIRD
General Motor's "F-cars" were the last of the big, gas-guzzling fastbacks. The Transam Firebird, with its 6.6-litre V-8 engine, was the king of them all.

Phoenix logo

CHEVROLET CAMARO
The Camaro was introduced in 1966 as General Motor's answer to the successful Ford Mustang. By the early 1970s, it had a ferocious racetrack record.

Electrically powered hood operates at touch of button

ASTON MARTIN V-8
One of the last front-engined, rear-wheel-drive supercars, the V-8 was Aston Martin's answer to the powerful Italian supercars of the late 1960s.

Power bulge needed to clear big V-8 engine's carburettors

Alloy body on fabricated steel chassis

FUTURE CLASSICS

THE PEOPLE WHO BUILT Bugattis and Bentleys before the Second World War would be amazed at the value of these "old cars" today. In the early 1990s, investors rushed to buy limited edition supercars knowing they could re-sell at a profit days later. That particular boom is over, but perhaps these cars will be the classics of tomorrow.

PORSCHE 959
In 1981, despite its high cost of £150,000, people still bought this 315 km/h (197 mph) twin-turbo supercar.

DODGE VIPER
Introduced in 1992 to much acclaim, the dramatic Dodge Viper became instantly collectible. Its 8-litre, 400 hp V-10 engine powers it from 0 to 100 km/h (60 mph) in under five seconds.

A 3.5-litre twin-turbo V-6 engine

FERRARI F40
For its fortieth anniversary, Ferrari unveiled the amazing F40. With its 478 bhp V-8 engine, it could hit 100 km/h (62 mph) in 4.8 seconds. This was the first of the 320-km/h (200-mph) supercars.

ASTON MARTIN ZAGATO
Aston Martin renewed old links with Italy's Zagato coachworks to build 50 of this 1985 lightweight two-seater. It has a powerful 430 bhp V-8 engine and is a rare sight on the road. Aston Martin built 50 convertibles as well.

CLASSIC FACTS

• A compressor in the Porsche 959 adjusts tyre pressures even at speed.

• The F40 has a bare carbon-fibre interior.

• The GTR's electronic brain steers the rear wheels separately.

NISSAN SKYLINE GTR
Starting with a capable but unexceptional coupé, Nissan fitted an electronic four-wheel drive, four-wheel steering, and traction system to produce a race winner that is also a high-tech pioneer.

JAGUAR XJ220
All 200 "supercats" were pre-sold and owners had to wait over two years for delivery. The 354-km/h (220-mph) luxury machines have earned prestige competing at Le Mans.

Alloy body with traditional oval grille

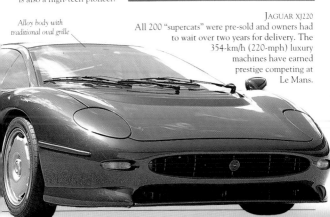

INTO THE FUTURE

UNUSUAL CARS

ADVERTISEMENT, experiment, a glimpse of the future – a car can be any of these things. Businesses use them to promote their products, engineers to try new ideas, and companies to test public reaction to new styles. Many of the more unusual cars will never be offered for sale, and some of the inventions cannot be used on the public road. But if it has wheels and an engine, it is nevertheless a car!

FRUIT SURPRISE
Underneath the fibreglass skin of this giant orange is the engine and transmission of a Mini. A fruit company built several of these eye-catchers in the 1970s.

TOMORROW'S CAR
Motor shows often feature radical "concept cars" like this to show new ideas in technology or styling. Usually, the ideas are toned down before production which may be several years in the future. Occasionally, public demand persuades a maker to put a new model in production quickly.

ALMOST TRUE
In the book and film *Chitty-Chitty-Bang-Bang*, the car could fly and swim as well as drive. Ian Fleming got the idea from 1920s racers built by Count Zborowski.

TOO SLOW, TOO SOON

British inventor Sir Clive Sinclair tried to get people to use small, clean, one-person vehicles in 1985. But his electric Sinclair C5 three-wheeler was slow and impractical, with a limited range and no weather protection. It was not a success.

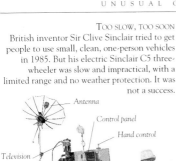

Antenna

Control panel

Hand control

Television camera

Fabric seats

Sample bags

Wire-mesh wheel

LUNAR ROVER

It cost $20 million to build four Lunar Rovers for the Apollo missions that explored the surface of the Moon. One of the Rovers set the Lunar Speed Record of 16.9 km/h (10.5 mph). The electric buggies had four-wheel drive, four-wheel steering, springy wire-mesh "tyres", and a range of 100 km (62 miles). The Rovers could also be folded away.

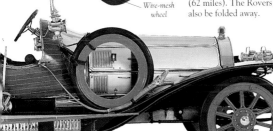

Chitty's wings fold under the boat body

DUAL-PURPOSE CARS

WHY BUY A CAR and a boat if your car can be made to swim? Many people have tried to combine two methods of transport to produce cars that fly, float, or can be driven on railway tracks. There was even a caravan that also functioned as a houseboat. But these experiments have rarely been successful.

VW SCHWIMMWAGEN
This military amphibian was developed before the famous Beetle became well known. It had the same suspension and running gear, but had four-wheel drive.

SUPERSUB
In the film *The Spy Who Loved Me*, Special Agent James Bond's Lotus Esprit swapped its wheels for fins and took to the sea. Sadly the car never existed; it was a radio-controlled model.

RAIL-ROVER
The Land-Rover has been adapted for hundreds of roles, including a fire-engine, a missile carrier, and a car-transporter. There have been versions with six wheels, tracks, and floats – and this one with removable rail wheels for use as a shunting engine.

PRIVATE AIRLINE
A successful attempt to make a car fly, the 1950s Aerocar could be fitted with wings, tail, and propeller at one airfield. It could then fly to another airfield, before finishing its journey by road towing the aeroparts behind.

Air-cooled engine in sealed compartment

Choice of six or eight wheels

Soft, ridged tyres act as "paddles"

GO ANYWHERE
The Crayford Argocat clambers over grass and mud with its eight fat tyres, and it can sail across water thanks to its fibreglass "bathtub" hull. It has a small two-stroke engine and basic controls.

MOTOR CRUISER
With its rear-mounted 1400 cc Triumph engine, the 1960s Amphicar reached 109 km/h (68 mph) on land, and 6 knots on water using twin propellers. It has been the best car-boat so far.

FUN ON WHEELS

CARS CAN BE FUN as well as useful. Owners decorate them, customize them, and tune them to make them stand out. A unique car can express the owner's personality, demonstrate his or her inventiveness, or prove his or her skill as an engineer. Some fun cars can be driven on the roads legally, while others are so unusual that they have to be transported to car shows or meetings on trailers.

TEST BED
Some one-off cars are built as show-pieces for an inventor's own ideas, like this one made to demonstrate the safety ideas of its American inventor.

BRIGHTENING IT UP
Even the most ordinary car becomes something special with a unique paint effect. You can get a specialist to air-brush a beautiful picture or do it yourself. Someone had fun paint-splashing this 2CV!

STAR CAR
Not many cars have become movie stars like Herbie the Beetle, who drove himself and even ran over water – thanks to clever film techniques!

ON THE STRIP
Drag racers have huge supercharged V-8 engines to fire them down a quarter-mile strip in a few seconds, reaching 500 km/h (300 mph) before popping parachutes in order to stop.

High wing stops tail lifting

Huge wheels for traction

1934 FORD SEDAN
Custom cars developed from early drag racers. Once this was an ordinary 1934 Ford. Now the roof is "chopped" low, and it has chromed low-riding suspension. With a 7.5-litre V-8 engine and fat wheels, acceleration is fierce.

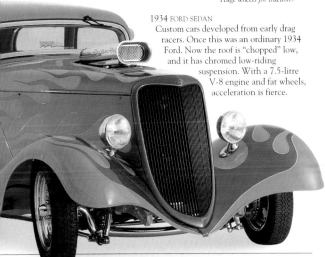

THINGS TO COME

Car can reach 32 km/h (20 mph)

WHAT WILL WE be driving in 50 years' time? Many of the "cars of the future" depicted 50 years ago were fanciful and seem comic to us now. The chances are that, apart from styling, the main changes in the 21st century will be navigational aids, new power units, and safety systems.

FOLDAWAY CAR
This neat idea comes from Japan, where parking is a problem. The petrol-engined three-wheeler folds into a suitcase to park in the office.

FOLLOW MY LEADER
To squeeze more cars safely onto existing roads, VW have tried linking several cars electronically. Only one driver actually drives.

FUTURE FACTS
• A single concept car can cost £1m and may only go a few kilometres.
• Some Japanese and German cars have satellite navigation.
• VW's Futura prototype parks itself.

Buttons to zoom map in or out

TRAFFIC NEWS
Electronic devices can warn drivers to avoid traffic jams. Overhead sensors on the road monitor traffic speed, and a control centre sends reports to the display panel in the car.

Flashing symbols show congested roads

OUT OF THIS WORLD
The Venus concept car will not appear on the roads –
the radical two-seater is a one-off. But such unusual
projects help push technical boundaries forward, and
test public opinion on inventive ideas and styling.

High-rise
doors

Wheels clothed
in smooth covers

ZOOM IN, ZOOM OUT
Renault tackled the parking
problem by suggesting a
"shrinking" vehicle. The
electric Zoom city-car
tucks in its rear
wheels when it
stops.

Car can reach 120
km/h (75 mph)
and recharges
in eight
hours

Wheels retracted
for parking

REFERENCE SECTION

TIMELINE OF CARS

The car has had a greater effect on our lives than any other invention, except, perhaps, the computer. First seen as a novelty, then a necessity, and now a global threat, its progress has been spectacular, though there have been few revolutionary advances of late.

1769			1895
1769–1849	1850–1879	1880–1890	1891–1895
PEOPLE, EVENTS, AND INVENTIONS — CUGNOT'S STEAM TRACTOR •1769 Nicholas Cugnot builds a steam-powered tractor – the world's first self-propelled road vehicle. •1833 A regular steam-coach service starts in Britain. •1847 Moses G. Farmer builds an experimental electric vehicle.	•1859 Etienne Lenoir develops a reliable gas-powered internal-combustion gas engine. •1865 Stephen Roper develops a practical steam wagon. •1876 Nikolaus Otto builds the first four-stroke-cycle engine.	•1885 Gottleib Daimler makes a petrol-driven motorcycle. •1886 Karl Benz's three-wheeler is the world's first true car. •1888 Benz makes the world's first car for commercial sale. •1889 Peugeot founded. BERSEY CAB	•1893 World's first number-plates are issued in France. •1895 The world's first official road race is held from Paris to Bordeaux and back. •1895 The Michelin brothers fit air-filled tyres to a Peugeot. •1895 De Dion Bouton begins selling petrol vehicles. •1895 Automobile Club de France is founded. •1895 Bersey electric cab invented.
WORLD EVENTS — •1770 James Cook sights Australia. •1776 American Declaration of Independence. •1789 French Revolution.	•1861–65 Civil War in the U.S.A. •1870 First African–Americans elected to U.S. Senate. •1871 Italy reunited as a single kingdom.	•1886 Gold rush in the Transvaal (now South Africa). •1890 Wounded Knee is the last battle between U.S. cavalry and Native Americans.	•1893 New Zealand is the first country to give women the right to vote in elections. •1894 War between Japan and China (ends 1895).

1896			1914
1896–1899	1900–1904	1905–1909	1910–1914

PEOPLE, EVENTS, AND INVENTIONS

HENRY FORD

- 1896 Henry Ford builds his first car.
- 1896 Oldsmobile founded.
- 1896 First London–Brighton run, to celebrate new British laws allowing speeds of 19 km/h (12 mph).
- 1898 Count Chasseloup-Laubat sets first speed record: 63 km/h (39 mph).
- 1899 Fiat and Renault founded.
- 1899 Camille Jenatzy reaches 106 km/h (66 mph) in an electric car.

- 1901 Daimler adopts Mercedes name.
- 1901 A Locomobile steamer conquers the 4,312 m (14,147 ft) Pikes Peak, Colorado, U.S.A.
- 1902 Cadillac founded.
- 1903 A Winton crosses the U.S.A. in 65 days.
- 1903 Ford Motor Company formed.
- 1903 Paris–Madrid race stopped after many deaths.
- 1903 Napier builds a 6-cylinder engine.
- 1903 V-8 engines appear in Europe.
- 1904 The U.S.A. overtakes France in car production.
- 1904 A racing Gobron-Brillé reaches 167 km/h (104 mph).

- 1906 Title "Grand Prix" used for the first time in France.
- 1906 Roadside fuel pumps appear.
- 1907 Brooklands Motor Course opens in Surrey, England.
- 1908 A Thomas Flyer wins the New York–Paris marathon.

MODEL T FORD

- 1908 Model T Ford introduced.
- 1908 A Talbot crosses Australia in 51 days.
- 1909 Automobiles Bugatti formed.
- 1909 Four-wheel brakes introduced by Arrol-Johnston.

- 1910 Overhead-cam engine used in Bugatti Brescia.
- 1910 Ferdinand Porsche wins the Prince Henry Trial in a Daimler.
- 1911 Chevrolet founded.
- 1911 Inaugural Monte Carlo Rally.
- 1912 Electric starters fitted to Cadillacs.
- 1913 Last Grand Prix victory by a chain-driven car (Mercedes).
- 1913 Ford's factory introduces a moving assembly line.
- 1914 First traffic lights, Cleveland, Ohio, U.S.A.

WORLD EVENTS

- 1896 First modern Olympic Games.
- 1899 War between Britain and Boer (Dutch) settlers in southern Africa (ends 1902).

- 1900 Boxer Rebellion in China against foreigners.
- 1903 The Wright *Flyer* makes the first controlled, powered flight in the U.S.A.

- 1905 Einstein's Theory of Relativity.
- 1906 Earthquake and fire devastate San Francisco, U.S.A.
- 1909 Bakelite is world's first plastic.

- 1912 African National Congress formed.
- 1914 Panama Canal opens.
- 1914 Start of First World War (ends 1918).

1915			1934
1915–1919	1920–1924	1925–1929	1930–1934

PEOPLE, EVENTS, AND INVENTIONS

1915–1919

- 1915 The Packard Twin Six is the first V-12 in production.
- 1916 First hill-climb race meeting held at Pike's Peak, Colorado, U.S.A.
- 1916 Vacuum-powered windscreen wiper invented. (Electric wipers follow in 1923.)
- 1917 Dodge uses all-steel bodies.
- 1919 The Eccles is the world's first production caravan.
- 1919 W.O. Bentley forms Bentley Motors.

RACING BENTLEY

- 1919 Paul Jaray uses Zeppelin wind-tunnel to test car aerodynamics.

1920–1924

- 1920 Duesenberg Model A is first car with hydraulic brakes.
- 1921 Ballot 2LS has twin-overhead-cam engine.
- 1921 56% of all cars are Ford Model Ts.
- 1921 Berlin's Avus Autobahn is world's first motorway.
- 1923 Lancia Lambda features integral body/chassis.
- 1923 Benz builds first mid-engined Grand Prix car.
- 1923 Leaded fuel goes on sale.
- 1924 Maxwell company renamed Chrysler.
- 1924 Cecil Kimber builds the first MG.
- 1924 Electric dipping headlamps devised in the U.S.A.

1925–1929

- 1925 Riding mechanics banned in Grand Prix.
- 1925 Czech armaments firm Skoda makes its first car, under licence from Spain's Hispano-Suiza.
- 1927 With more than 15 million built, production of Model T Fords ceases.
- 1927 Car radios are widely available.
- 1927 Henry Segrave reaches 328 km/h (204 mph) in a Sunbeam car.
- 1929 Five million new cars are made in the U.S.A. this year.
- 1929 Syncromesh gearbox standard on Cadillac cars.
- 1929 Production of the Ford Model A reaches 1 million in only 15 months.

1930–1934

- 1930 Bugatti creates the Royale.

V-16 CADILLAC

- 1930 Cadillac offers the first V-16 engine.
- 1931 Rolls-Royce takes over Bentley.
- 1932 Alfa Romeo P3 is the first single-seat Grand Prix car.
- 1933 World's first drive-in cinema opens in the U.S.A.
- 1934 Citroën's pioneering Traction Avant has front-wheel drive and a monocoque body.
- 1934 Paul Jaray's aerodynamic Tatra saloon has a record low drag of Cd 0.34.
- 1934 Chrysler's aerodynamic Airflow saloon introduced.

WORLD EVENTS

1915–1919

- 1916 Irish uprising against British rule.
- 1917 Ras Tafari emperor of Ethiopia.
- 1918 Bolsheviks gain power in Russian Revolution.

1920–1924

- 1920 Mahatma Gandhi leads peaceful mass protests against British rule in India.
- 1921 Irish Free State estsblished.
- 1922 USSR formed.

1925–1929

- 1926 General Strike in Britain.
- 1929 Crash of the U.S.A.'s Wall Street stock exchange triggers world economic depression.

1930–1934

- 1930 The planet Pluto is discovered.
- 1931 Nazi leader Adolf Hitler becomes German Chancellor.
- 1932 Empire State Building completed.

1935			1954
1935–1939	1940–1944	1945–1949	1950–1954

PEOPLE, EVENTS, AND INVENTIONS

• 1935 Windscreen washers offered on Triumph cars. • 1935 World's first parking meters, Oklahoma City, U.S.A. • 1935 Public unpopularity forces Chrysler to restyle the Airflow. • 1936 Mercedes introduces the first private diesel car. • 1936 Dual-circuit brakes installed in Hudson cars. • 1936 First Morgan four-wheeler. • 1936 Prototypes of the Volkswagen Beetle produced. • 1937 G.E.T. Eyston's *Thunderbolt* exceeds 500 km/h (312 mph). • 1939 Packard introduces air-conditioning.	U.S. JEEP • 1940 U.S. Army takes delivery of its first four-wheel-drive General Purpose cars, or "Jeeps". • 1940 Oldsmobile offers the first fully automatic gearboxes. • 1940 A streamlined BMW wins the Mille Miglia race. It has a significant influence on post-war design. • 1940 Car factories in Western countries are used to produce war machinery. • 1941 The military Kubelwagen jeep and the amphibious Schwimmwagen are the first Volkswagens in production.	• 1945 Volkswagen production restarts under British army control. • 1947 Bristol's first car borrows BMW technology as part of war reparations. • 1947 The first Ferrari enters a race. • 1948 Land-Rover introduced. • 1948 Jaguar XK120 is the sensation of the London Motor show. • 1948 The 356 is the first car to bear the name Porsche. • 1948 Lincoln and Cadillac introduce electric windows. • 1948 Drag-racing strips open in California. • 1949 Disc brakes available on Chryslers. • 1949 The Citroën 2CV is launched.	• 1950 Giuseppe Farina is first World Champion Driver. • 1951 Ford pioneers crash-testing in U.S.A. • 1951 Chrysler offers power-steering. • 1951 "People's car" is the first Chinese car in production. • 1951 Crash-helmet is now compulsory in international racing. • 1953 World Sports Car Championship inaugurated. • 1953 Chevrolet Corvette goes on sale. • 1953 Michelin develops radial tyre. • 1954 Mercedes uses fuel injection on the 300SL. MERCEDES 300SL

WORLD EVENTS

• 1936 Spanish Civil War begins (ends 1939). • 1939 Germany invades Poland, starting Second World War (ends 1945).	• 1941 U.S.A. enters Second World War, after Japanese attack on Pearl Harbor. • 1944 Allied invasion of Europe heralds end of war.	• 1947 British rule of India ends. • 1948 State of Israel formed in Palestine. • 1949 Chairman Mao declares China a People's Republic.	• 1950 Korean War begins (ends 1953). • 1953 Scientists discover structure of DNA, which controls the genetic make-up of living creatures.

1955			1974
1955–1959	1960–1964	1965–1969	1970–1974

PEOPLE, EVENTS, AND INVENTIONS

- 1955 Stirling Moss wins the Mille Miglia at a record speed.
- 1955 Worst ever racing crash kills 84 people at Le Mans.
- 1957 Seat-belts are offered on all new Volvo cars.
- 1957 The Italian government bans the Mille Miglia after two competitors and 12 spectators are killed.
- 1958 Lotus Elite is first fibreglass monocoque car.
- 1959 Four-way hazard flashers fitted to Chrysler cars.
- 1959 The Austin Mini revolutionizes the design of small cars.
- 1959 Ford has now made more than 50 million vehicles.

- 1960 Last ever Grand Prix victory by a front-engined car (Ferrari).
- 1962 Lotus 25 is first monocoque Grand Prix car.
- 1962 Industrial designer Raymond Loewy styles Studebaker's Avanti.
- 1963 NSU Spyder is the first car with a rotary, or "Wankel", engine.
- 1964 Porsche 911 introduced.
- 1964 Donald Campbell achieves 648 km/h (403 mph) in *Bluebird II*.

AMPHICAR

- 1965 Two Amphicars cross the English Channel.
- 1965 Craig Breedlove reaches 967 km/h (601 mph) in the jet-propelled *Spirit of America*.
- 1965 A gas-turbine driven Rover finishes tenth at Le Mans.
- 1966 Chaparral 2F sports racing car is first to have aerofoils.
- 1968 Ford offer anti-lock brakes.
- 1968 The advanced rotary-engined Ro80 is launched by NSU.
- 1968 America builds its 250 millionth car.

CAMPBELL'S RECORD-BREAKING *BLUEBIRD II*

- 1971 Treadless ("slick") racing tyres introduced.
- 1971 The $5 million electric Lunar Rover is the first car on the moon.
- 1973 Electronic ignition introduced on Chryslers.
- 1973 The first air-bags are offered by General Motors.
- 1973 Matra's fibreglass monocoque Bagheera offers three seats abreast.
- 1973 As fuel prices soar, smaller, more efficient cars increase in popularity.
- 1974 The first turbocharged car in production is the BMW 2002 Turbo.
- 1974 Solid-state instrumentation is featured on Aston-Martin Lagonda.

WORLD EVENTS

- 1956 Pakistan is first Islamic republic.
- 1956 USSR crushes anti-communist uprising in Hungary.
- 1957 Treaty of Rome creates E.E.C.

- 1961 Yuri Gagarin is first man in space.
- 1962 Cuban Missile Crisis.
- 1963 U.S. President John F. Kennedy assassinated.

- 1965 Vietnam War begins (ends 1975).
- 1968 Revolution in Czechoslovakia put down by USSR.
- 1969 Apollo 11 lands on the moon.

- 1973 Yom Kippur War between Arabs and Israelis.
- 1973 Oil crisis in West, as Arab states cut oil supplies and raise prices.

1975			1995
1975–1979	1980–1984	1985–1989	1990–1995

PEOPLE, EVENTS, AND INVENTIONS

PORSCHE 911

• 1975 The Porsche Turbo becomes the world's fastest accelerating road-car.

• 1976 Tyrrell's P34 is the only six-wheeled car to win a Grand Prix race.

• 1977 Tom Sneva achieves first 320 km/h (200 mph) lap at Indianapolis.

• 1977 Renault uses turbochargers in its Grand Prix engines.

• 1977 Lotus 78 is first "ground effect" racing car: air rushing under its low "skirt" holds it firmly on to the road.

• 1978 In England, a solar-powered car reaches 13 km/h (8 mph).

• 1981 Colin Chapman's ingenious twin-chassis Lotus 88 banned from racing.

• 1981 First (and so far only) car with a stainless steel body – the DeLorean.

• 1982 Audi 100 has a drag of Cd 0.30, the lowest ever figure for a production car.

• 1982 VW Beetle surpasses Model T Ford production.

• 1983 Richard Noble's jet-powered *Thrust II* sets new record of 1,019 km/h (633 mph).

• 1983 BMW's four-cylinder F1 turbo engine is capable of 1,000 bhp.

• 1985 Renault uses pneumatic valves in Grand Prix engines.

• 1986 New circuit record of 376 km/h (234 mph) set by Rick Mears.

• 1986 BMW displays the Z1 sports car, with its plastic body and drop-down doors: public demand forces it into production.

• 1987 Lotus develops "active ride" suspension.

FERRARI F40

• 1988 Ferrari F40 is the first of several road cars capable of more than 320 km/h (200 mph).

• 1990 General Motors' battery-powered Impact car can travel for 190 km (120 miles) at 88 km/h (55 mph) without recharging.

• 1991 Al Teague sets a new record for wheel-driven cars at 660 km/h (410 mph).

• 1992 Al Unser Jr completes the hat-trick of Unsers who have won the Indy 500, alongside father Al Unser Snr and brother Bobby.

• 1992 Ferrari enters its 500th Grand Prix.

• 1993 McLaren F1 is first road car with carbon-fibre monocoque body.

WORLD EVENTS

• 1976 First "test-tube baby" born. • 1976 Viking 1 lands on Mars. • 1979 USSR invades Afghanistan.	• 1980 Iran–Iraq War begins (ends 1988). • 1981 Scientists identify AIDS virus. • 1984 Famine in Ethiopia.	• 1986 Protests by students in favour of democracy crushed by Chinese authorities. • 1989 Communist regimes in Eastern Europe collapse.	• 1990 East and West Germany reunited. • 1991 Gulf War. • 1993 First free, multi-racial elections in South Africa.

INVENTORS AND CREATORS

Few cars are built by just one person, but sometimes one person provides the driving force that changes the way things are done. The men on these pages played a significant role in the history of the car. Some are household names; others are now forgotten.

GOTTLIEB DAIMLER (1834–1900)
Daimler's experiments led to the first petrol engine in 1883, and a petrol-driven motorcycle in 1885. He licensed and sold a range of engines for boats, trains, and cars, and with Wilhelm Maybach invented the carburettor.

HENRY FORD (1863–1947)
Ford's aim was for everyone to afford a simple car. His innovations came in production, not design – the Model T was out-dated before it ceased production. The American Ford Motor Co. became one of the world's giant companies.

KARL BENZ (1844–1929)
Called "the father of the automobile", Benz's three-wheeler led to the world's first production car, the Velo of 1894. By 1900, Benz & Co. had built over 1,700 cars. The firm joined with Daimler in 1926 to produce Mercedes-Benz.

FREDERICK LANCHESTER (1874–1970)
Lanchester's car designs were visionary, including an integral chassis/body. But the public did not like the bonnetless shape, and his brother George's more conventional cars sustained the company until 1956.

HENRY ROYCE (1863–1933)
Together with Charles Rolls (1877–1910), this Englishman created "the best car in the world". His exacting standards resulted in quality cars. He lived the later part of his life in France, where prototypes were driven for inspection.

FERDINAND PORSCHE (1875–1951)
Apart from the famous sports cars, Professor Porsche's inventive skills produced the magnificent Mercedes SS, the Volkswagen Beetle, the Auto-Union racing cars – and the Second World War Panzer tank.

THE RENAULT BROTHERS

Louis Renault (1877–1944), with his brothers Marcel and Fernand, sold his first cars in 1899, and went on to influence European car development through a huge range of models. Racing successes helped, but Marcel was killed in the 1903 Paris–Madrid race. Nationalized in 1945, Renault remains one of France's biggest companies.

ANDRE CITROEN (1878–1935)

Inspired by Ford, in 1918 Citroën turned his armaments factories in France to car production. A skilled manager and engineer, he brought motoring to millions in Europe. The 1934 Traction Avant was ahead of its time.

ENZO FERRARI (1898–1989)

Ferrari's passion for motor-racing dominated the cars he built in Italy after running the successful Alfa-Romeo team in the 1930s. Ferraris have won many Grand Prix, but Enzo refused to visit the races his cars entered.

ETTORE BUGATTI (1881–1947)

Surrounded by an artistic family and obsessed by engineering elegance, Bugatti created exquisite French cars which are highly prized today. Examples are the Type 35 racing car and the 1929 Royale – "the Car of Kings".

COLIN CHAPMAN (1928–1982)

The founder of Lotus Cars, Chapman invented brilliant lightweight suspensions, chassis, and engines. The British Lotus has won many Grand Prix, and the road cars are famed for their delicate handling.

WALTER OWEN BENTLEY (1888–1971)

Bugatti's great British rival, Bentley built solid, powerful sports machines which won Le Mans five times. Though his original company went out of business in 1930, the name Bentley continues as part of Rolls-Royce, and his beautifully built cars are still raced today.

FAMOUS RACES AND PLACES

Since the invention of the car, drivers have competed to be first and fastest. Cars have moved from hand-throttles to computer control and on-board cameras, but racing still needs skill and daring. Compared to the risky road races of Edwardian times, today's circuits are safe, but often not as colourful as some of history's famous races.

PARIS–MADRID RACE 1903

The last of the great Edwardian open-road races, this French event stopped when it reached Bordeaux after dozens of competitors and spectators had been killed. There were few safety measures and onlookers did not expect the speeds of up to 145 km/h (90 mph). After this, races were held on roads closed to other traffic, or on purpose-built tracks.

DAYTONA BEACH

With its enormous stretches of smooth sand, Daytona Beach in the U.S.A. has hosted many speed record attempts. In 1906, a Stanley steamer took the Land Speed Record at 194.51 km/h (121.5 mph). By 1936, the 480-km/h (300-mph) record-breakers had moved elsewhere, so the town built a successful sand race-track. Since 1959, a banked circuit nearby has hosted the tough 500-mile and 24-hour races.

MONACO GRAND PRIX

Every year since 1929, Monte Carlo's famous Formula One race has closed the centre of the Mediterranean town for four days in May. Overtaking is extremely hard on the narrow track, one of the few street circuits still in use. It is the only Grand Prix circuit that includes a tunnel.

MILLE MIGLIA

This road race became one of Italy's great annual festivals. From the first race in 1927, sports cars set off at one-minute intervals on the 1,600-km (1,000-mile) route from Brescia across tortuous mountain passes to Rome and back to Brescia. The last Mille Miglia was in 1957, when a Ferrari crashed into the crowd, killing many people. Today there is an annual re-enactment featuring historic cars.

BROOKLANDS RACING CIRCUIT

The world's first race-track, Brooklands was built in 1907 both for testing new cars and for racing. Drivers broke many records on the banked British course, peaking in 1935 at 229.4 km/h (143.3 mph) – a record set by John Cobb's 24-litre aero-engined Napier Railton. Although Brooklands closed in 1939, part of the track remains as a museum of motoring.

1950S COOPER

INDIANAPOLIS 500 RACE

The 800-km (500-mile) race round the "Brickyard" (when it opened in 1909 it was paved with bricks instead of boards) is a gruelling feat. This American classic attracts hundreds of thousands of spectators to the track. It is also the fastest race anywhere – the 750 bhp machines streak round at over 300 km/h (190 mph), barely slowing on the four steeply-banked left-hand corners.

LE MANS 24-HOUR RACE

First begun in 1924 as a test for touring cars, this French endurance marathon (around a circuit normally open to traffic) remains one of the toughest challenges for today's sports cars. Until safety chicanes were introduced in 1990, cars reached speeds of 370 km/h (230 mph) on the famous Mulsanne Straight. Cafés and a funfair stay open all night.

SHELSLEY WALSH

Only 1073 m (3520 ft) long, this scenic hill-climb is the world's oldest motor sport venue still in use. Road racing has long been banned in Britain, so from 1905 onwards everything from road-cars to Grand Prix racers has roared up this private drive. Ninety years ago, the record for the climb was 55 seconds; now it is half that, achieved by specially designed machines.

AMAZING CAR FACTS

The excitement of competition, incredible technical advances, and the desire for fame have inspired great feats, odd ideas, and strange devices. Some are in record books; some are historical footnotes.

DE DION BOUTON
MODEL Q

POWER-HUNGRY

Until the turbocharged cars of the 1980s began to reach 1000 bhp, the most powerful Grand Prix car of all was the Mercedes-Benz W125 of 1937. Its supercharged engine put out 600 bhp.

MASS TRANSPORT

By 1900, the French car makers De Dion had built over 22,000 engines. Most of the engines were sold to other car makers, but De Dion also produced about 200 of its own vehicles per month.

TWIST AND TURN

The closed racing circuit with the most bends was the original Nürburgring in the Eifel mountains in Germany. Its best-known 22.78-km (14.17-mile) version involved 176 bends in the road.

FAMILY TRIUMPH

Pike's Peak is a 20-km (12.4-mile) hill-climb in the U.S.A. which rises 1,500 m (4,918 ft) above sea-level. In 1916, the winning time was almost 21 minutes; today, the record is just over 11 minutes. Members of the Unser family have won the race 30 times since Louis Unser's triumph in 1934.

SOUND BARRIER

Although Richard Noble holds the official Land Speed Record at 1019.24 km/h (633.46 mph), Stan Barrett claims to be the first man to exceed the speed of sound on land in 1980, at mach 1.01 (1190.1 km/h or 739.6 mph).

RICHARD NOBLE AND THRUST II

FORD GT40

FAST AND FURIOUS
At the 1971 Grand Prix at Monza, Peter Gethin won at 242.62 km/h (150.67 mph). The fastest races are on America's banked tracks, with speeds of up to 377 km/h (234.28 mph).

VEE FOR VICTORY
The most successful racing engine is the Cosworth DFV, made in England. From 1967 to 1983 it won 155 Grand Prix. Over 400 were built.

LEFT IS RIGHT
Sweden switched from driving on the left to the right one day in 1967, and there were fewer accidents than usual. Pre-war Bugattis had right-hand drive though cars are driven on the right in France.

COME AGAIN
Only two cars have won the Le Mans 24-hour race twice – a Ford GT40 in 1968 and 1969, and a Porsche 956 in 1985 and 1986. The only car to compete at Le Mans three times is the 1938 Bentley "Embiricos" saloon, in 1949, 1950, and 1951.

CAUGHT ON FILM
In Paris in 1900, the French police tested a camera that snapped a sequence of shots to confirm the speed of passing motorcars.

PROP FORWARD
Frenchman Marcel Leyat thought cars should be propeller-driven. In the 1920s, he sold a number with a caged front prop, aeroplane-like body, and rear-wheel steering. There were open and delivery van versions, too. A few still exist.

ON THE BUTTON
The first electric starter was on the American 1909 Standard. All Cadillacs had them from 1912, though pneumatic starters were already available on Wolseley and Minerva cars.

NO VISITORS
In 1976, angry workers at a French textile plant broke into a sealed shed to discover that their bosses, the Schlumpf brothers, had for years been buying fine vintage cars. There were over 120 Bugattis alone. The large building is now a national museum.

LEYAT'S PROPELLER-DRIVEN CAR

RESOURCES

MUSEUMS

UNITED KINGDOM
Brooklands Museum
Brooklands Road,
Weybridge, Surrey
KT13 0QN
Tel: 01932 857381
Fax: 01932 855465

**The Donington
Collection**
Castle Donington,
Derby DE7 2RP
Tel: 01332 810048

Heritage Motor Centre
Banbury Road, Gaydon,
Warks CV35 0BJ
Tel: 01926 641188

Midland Motor Museum
Stourbridge Road,
Stourbridge
Salop
WV15 6DT

**National Motor
Museum**
Beaulieu, Hants
SO42 7ZN
Tel: 01590 612345

AUSTRIA
**Vienna Technical
Museum**
Mariahilfe Strasse 212,
1140 Wien
Tel: 0222 891010

BELGIUM
Autoworld
Centre Mondiale de
l'Automobile, Esplanade
du Cinquantenaire 11,
1041 Bruxelles
Tel: 02 736 41 65

DENMARK
Jysk Automobilmuseum
DK-8883, Gjern
Tel: 8687 50 50

FINLAND
Vehoniemi Car Museum
SF-36570 Kaivanto
Tel: 358 31 767 794

FRANCE
**Collection des voitures
du Prince de Monaco**
Les Terrasses de
Fontvieille,
98000 Monaco
Tel: 93 30 42 27

Le Mans Museum
Circuit des 24 Heures
du Mans, BP424,
72009 Le Mans
Tel: 43 72 72 24

Museum Peugeot
L'Aventure Peugeot,
25600 Sochaux
Tel: 81 94 48 21

Schlumpf Collection
192 Avenue de Colmar,
68100 Mulhouse
Tel: 89 42 29 17

GERMANY
BMW Museum
Petuelring 130,
BMW-Haus,
8000 Munchen 40
Tel: 0893895

Daimler-Benz Museum
Postfach 60 02 02, 7000
Stuttgart 60
Tel: 0711 172 2578

Mercedes-Benz Museum
Untertürkheim,
Stuttgart
Tel: 711 172 2915

Porsche Museum,
Porschestrasse 42, 7000
Stuttgart-Zuffenhausen
Tel: 0711 827 5685

Rosso-Bianco Collection
Obernauerstrasse 125,
8750 Aschaffenburg
Tel: 06021 21358

HOLLAND
**National Motor
Museum**
Steuweg 8, 4941 VR
Raamsdonksveer
Tel: 01 621 85400

ITALY
Alfa Romeo Museum
Via Santa Maria Rossa,
20020 Arese, Milano

Centro Storico Fiat
Via Chiabrera 20,
Torino
Tel: 670 474

Ferrari Factory Museum
Via Abatone, Maranello
Tel: 21 74 55

**Padiglione Automobili
d'Epoca**
Autodromo Nazionale,
Monza, Milano
Tel: 3922 366

**Turin Automobile
Museum (Biscaretti)**
Corso Unita d'Italia 40,
Torino
Tel: 677 666

JAPAN
**Kawaguchiko Motor
Museum**
(Harada Collection)
Tel: 05558 63511

PORTUGAL
Museo de Caramulo
3475 Caramula
Tel: 032 86270

U.S.A.
Behring Museum
3750 Blackhawk Plaza
Circle, Danville,
California 94506
Tel: 510 736 2277

Henry Ford Museum
20900 Oakwood Blvd,
Dearborn,
Michigan 48121
Tel: 313 271 1620

**Indianapolis Speedway
Hall of Fame**
4790 West 16th St,
Indianapolis,
Indiana 46222
Tel: 317 248 6747

**National Automobile
Museum**
(Harrah Collection)
10 Lake St. South,
Nevada 89501
Tel: 702 333 9300

SPORTING
BODIES

**Antique Automobile
Club of America**
501 West Governor
Road, PO Box 417,
Hershey, Pennsylvania
17033, U.S.A.
Tel: 717 534 1910

CART/Indycar Inc.
390 Enterprise Court,
Bloomfield Hills, MI
48302, U.S.A.
Tel: 810 334 8500

**Fédération
Internationale de
l'Automobile (FIA)**
8 Place de la Concorde,
75008 Paris, France
Tel: 142 65 99 51

**RAC Motor Sports
Association**
Motor Sports House,
Riverside Park,
Colnbrook, Slough
SL3 0HG
Tel: 0175 3681736

Vintage Sports Car Club
121 Russell Road,
Newbury, Berks
Tel: 01635 44411

Glossary

AIRBAG
A tough balloon, usually hidden in the steering wheel, which, in an accident, inflates to protect occupants of car.

ANTI-SKID BRAKES (ABS)
Electronic system which releases the brakes if a wheel locks, to prevent skidding.

AXLE
Originally a beam or tube which carried the front or rear wheels. Today, used to mean the front or rear suspension.

bhp
Brake horsepower, originally hp. Most common measure of engine power.

BUCKET SEAT
Sports car seat which curves around the hips and shoulders to hold driver in place.

CAMSHAFT
Revolving shaft carrying shaped discs called "cams" which push open the valves.

CARBURETTOR
Device that mixes air and fuel together by suction to make the inflammable mixture that produces a car's power.

CATALYTIC CONVERTER
Fitted into the exhaust pipe, the "cat" helps to convert some noxious gases to harmless ones.

CHASSIS
Originally the wood or metal frame of a car on which the running-gear and body were mounted. Now used to refer to the running-gear of a car.

CHOKE
Carburettor mechanism which enriches the fuel-air mix for cold starting.

CLUTCH
Means of disconnecting the engine from the gearbox, to allow changing gear and coming to a halt without stopping the engine.

COMPACT
Small four-person car, but larger than a Mini.

CONCEPT CAR
A one-off design, built to display at car shows and gauge public opinion on new ideas.

CONVERTIBLE
Car with a fold-away roof. Also known as soft-top, cabriolet, drop-head.

CRANKSHAFT
Drives the clutch and therefore the wheels.

CRUMPLE ZONE
To protect the occupants, the front and rear of all modern cars are designed to crumple, or collapse progressively in an accident.

CUSTOM-BUILT
Anything which is tailor-made for a specific client.

CUSTOMIZED
A car which has been converted from standard for visual effect.

DAMPER
Hydraulic device attached to each corner of the suspension. It allows slow movement, but restricts rapid motion. Used to prevent wheel bouncing rapidly.

DIFFERENTIAL
Device that splits engine power unequally between the inner and outer driving wheels on a corner, as the outer wheel has further to travel.

DISC BRAKES
System in which two pads of friction material clamp on a large flat metal disc attached to the wheels to slow a car.

DRUM BRAKES
Curved "shoes" of friction material press against the inside rim of a shallow brake drum to slow the car.

ERGONOMICS
The science of making seating, handles, and driver controls comfortable, and easy to use and understand.

FLOORPAN
Pressed steel floor of car that carries the running-gear.

FORMULA
For fair competition, all racing cars must conform to a formula or set of rules.

FOUR-BY-FOUR, OR 4X4
Four-wheeled vehicle on which all four wheels are powered.

FOUR-STROKE ENGINE
The cycle of four actions common to most petrol engines: induction, compression, ignition, exhaust.

FUEL INJECTION
Modern alternative to the carburettor.

IGNITION SYSTEM
The complete electrical circuitry which explodes the fuel – includes battery, alternator, coil, distributor, spark plugs.

PACE-NOTES
Accurate notes about course made by rally co-driver and read to driver during rally.

PITS
Row of workshops where racing cars can stop for repairs or refuelling during a race.

RACK-AND-PINION
Steering system using toothed gear (the pinion) on the steering column to slide a toothed "rack" left and right to turn the wheels.

RAID
Long-distance off-road endurance rally.

RV
Recreational vehicle – American term for a large motor-home.

SHOCK-ABSORBER
See DAMPER

SPOILER
Aerodynamic panel which alters, or "spoils" the airflow. Used to reduce drag.

SUPERCHARGER
A pump driven by the engine which forces more air/fuel mixture into the cylinder to increase power.

SUSPENSION
The system that connects the wheels to the shell, and flexes to absorb bumps.

THROTTLE
Means of controlling the engine's speed by regulating amount of air/fuel delivered.

VEE-ENGINE (V-6 ETC)
An engine with two banks of cylinders in a V-shape, with a central crankshaft.

VETERAN CAR
A car built before 1905.

VINTAGE CAR
A car built between 1919 and 1930.

Index

Acknowledgements

Dorling Kindersley would like to thank:
Hilary Bird; Kate Eager; Joseph Hoyle; and
Auberon Hedgecoe; Kevin Ryan; and Ron
Cordani and John Hannah of the BBC.

Photographs by: Simon Clay; Andy
Crawford; Mike Dunning; Linton
Gardiner; Ralph Hall; Dave King; John
Lepine; Dave Rudkin; Tim Ridley; Clive
Streeter; Karl Stone; Matthew Ward; Andy
Willshire; Jerry Young

Illustrations by: David Ashby; Alan
Austin; Stephen Biesty; Steve Bull; Stan
Cephas Johnson; Mike Gillah; Nick
Goodall; John Hutchinson; Jason Lewis

Picture Credits
t top; *c* centre; *a* above, *b* below; *l* left; *r* right.
The Publisher would like to thank the
following for their kind permission to
reproduce their photographs:
Action Plus 96cr; The Advertising
Archives 21tl, 27tr, 30tr; Aeroplane
Monthly/Richard Riding 131tr; Audi 65cr;
Jane Ayers PR and Marketing 13cl; BBC
90tr, 91tl; BMW 54tr; The Bridgeman Art
Library/National Railway Museum, York
17tr; British Motor Industry Heritage Trust
38b, 93b, 96tl, 130bl; Britax / Hytner
Anderson 51br, 94cl; J. Allen Cash 31tl;
David Chapman 126-127, 131bl, 142tr;
Lester Cheeseman 22bl; Crayford Special
Equipment Ltd. 131c; Gordon Cruikshank
83b, 107tl, 117b; Daimler 63br; Downtown
News Service/Jerry Ames 76c;
Environmental Picture Library/Jimmy
Holmes 53tl, tr, /Robert Brook br, /Leslie
Garland 57tr; Mary Evans Picture Library
14-15b, 81c; Fiat/D.S.A Ltd. 26bl, 26cl,
37cr, 73cr, 77t, cl, 87cr; Ford U.K. Ltd.
21tr, 22br, 27br, 48b, 49tl, tr, cl, 50b, 51cl,
141tl; The Ronald Grant Archive 95tr,
130cr, 133t; Robert Harding Picture Library
13tr, 23cr, 64cl, br, 88-89, 90tr, 91tl, 92tr,
/Ian Griffiths 93tr, 93cl, 95t, 95br, 97tl;
Hulton Deustch Collection 12tl, 14cl; The
Image Bank 12b, /Nick Pavloff 56br, 91b;
Mansell Collection 14cl, 144tr, cl;
Mathewson Bull 75tl, 100tr; Mazda 134tl;
Mercedes Benz 52tl, 65b, 80tl, 118tl;
Michelin 45br; Motor Industry Archive/
Mazda 24c, /Mondeo br, /Hyundai 25br,
113bl, 128bl; The Motoring Picture Library,
National Motor Museum, Beaulieu 7br, 19tr
20bl, 22cr, 32-33, 50tl, 60tl, 61tl, cr, 65tl,
66br, 67cl, br, 70tr, 70bl, 72cr, 74cr, 92br,
83c, 85cr, 94-95b, 103cr, 109t, 115b, 116tl,
cl, b, 117tl, c, 124tr, cl, bl, 128tl, 130tl,
133cr, 139tl, 140tr, 143br, 144tl, cr, bl, br,
145tl, cla, cra, crb, clb, br; NASA 129c;
Nissan 24tl, 29tr, 125cr; Pictor 40tl, 52-53b;
Quadrant Picture Library 26br, 28cl, 31tr, b
49br, 60cr, 61bl, br, 63cr, 66tr, c, 71t, 72b,
78-79, 82tl, cr, bl, 84tr, cl, 84-85b, 85br,
86tl, b, 87tr, 101tl, 103tl, 104tl, 105t, 105c,
108br, 110-111, 112cl, 112br, 113tr, 114tl,
115tr, 119tl, cr, 125tl, b, 129tr, 146-147c;
Range/Bettman Archive 21cl; Reader's
Digest, Australia 74cl; Renault/Publicis 30bl
br, 48tr, 74-75b, 73cl, br, 135b; Rex Feature
55cr, 60bl, 64tr, 67cr, 83t, 85tl, 101tc, 102cl
104b, 109cr, 148br; Sporting Pictures 98-99,
100bl, 103br, 106b, tr; Tony Stone
Images/Anthony Cassidy 56l, /Pete Seaward
57l, 57b, 88-89, 97b; Traffic Master Ltd.
134b; Suzuki/Farquar PR 81b, 92cl; Vauxhall
70br; Volkswagen 75br, cr, tr, 76c, 134br;
Volvo 51tr; Warfield Productions 128-129;
ZEFA 13br, 70cl, 71bl, 72tr, 132cl, 132bl.

Every effort has been made to trace the copyright
holders and we apologise in advance for any
unintentional omissions.